Nets, Lines and Pots

Dedicated to all New Zealand fishermen, past and present.

Nets, Lines and Pots

A history of New Zealand fishing vessels

–VOLUME ONE–

Emmanuel Makarios

IPL Books

First Published in 1996 by:

IPL Books
P.O. Box 10-215
Wellington
New Zealand

In association with:

The Wellington Maritime Museum
P.O. Box 893
Wellington

Copyright © 1996 Emmanuel Makarios

ISBN 0-908876-98-X

Art Director: Geoffrey B. Churchman
Pre-Press Production by IPL Publishing Services, Wellington
Printed in Hong Kong through IPL Print Services

Metric Conversion Factors

1 foot (ft) = 305 mm	1 pound (lb) = 0.46 kg	1 gallon = 4.55 litres
1 land mile = 1.61 km	1 sea mile = 1.83 km	1 knot = 1 sea mile/hr

In keeping with the modern convention, vessels are treated as gender-neutral.

Half title: Sunset atmosphere on board a trawler in the 1960s. (Wellington Maritime Museum Collection)
Title page: The trawler *Maimai* sails up Wellington Harbour. (National Archives Collection, AAQT 6401 A69 747)

Contents

Preface	6
Introduction	7
The *Janie Seddon* and the early years of Talley's Fisheries	12
Pioneer fishermen of Island Bay	20
The early fishermen of Paremata's Hobson Street remembered	34
Alan Aberdein – Blue cod & crayfishing in the Chathams	44
Trawlers at war	55
Maimai – from warship to trawler	63
The life of the *Thomas Currell*	69
The early years of commercial fishing in Taranaki	77
The middle years of commercial fishing in Taranaki	86
Captain Charles Daniel: Master mariner – Fisheries Inspector	95
The *Mobil Chatham*	103
The *Nora Niven* – a pioneer	108
Acknowledgements	111
The author	112

Preface

In researching and writing these articles, Emmanuel Makarios, and his employer, the Wellington Maritime Museum, are providing a valuable service to current and future generations of New Zealanders. The citizens of any country are only able to read and be aware of their history, and how their various cultures developed, because someone took the trouble to record the events of today for tomorrow. Emmanuel's research, including oral histories, is a very timely attempt to provide a record before time obliterates the evidence.

I say timely because, in a sense, Emmanuel is in a race against time in that many of the fishing industry's founder members are nearing the end of their days. When they pass on, the rich fabric of experience contained in their memories dies with them.

Formal historical events born out of political and legislative processes are well recorded as factual data, but the living experiences and endeavours of the individual are not so well attended to. Likewise the individual's items of memorabilia and photographs are often lost with the passage of time. Quite often the value of such items is not appreciated by the individual's heirs and become scattered or lost altogether. Hopefully Emmanuel and the Wellington Maritime Museums can in large part arrest that loss.

As editor of *Seafood New Zealand* where Emmanuel's articles appear in a regular monthly format, I receive an overwhelming number of sincerely favourable comments extolling the virtues of this work. With his easy to read style and human touch, Emmanuel has a much larger and more appreciative audience than his modesty would allow him to believe.

Even if the interviews undertaken by Emmanuel are not written up and published immediately, they remain secure on tape for future action. Likewise photographs and documents can be professionally recorded, filed and/or displayed by the museum. The compilation of Emmanuel's fishing industry historical articles to date in this publication will bring an interesting view of part of our relatively short history to many more New Zealanders than have read the monthly versions in *Seafood New Zealand*. Many readers will find that they will be familiar with, or have heard of the characters depicted and the events and boats described. The fact that the individuals involved come from a wide range of different ethnic backgrounds adds an overlay of aura to these accounts.

I sincerely hope that this volume is followed by many more to make up a complete series on the human side of New Zealand's fishing history. Emmanuel has made a great start and deserves our help and encouragement because there's a lot more to tell yet.

Peter Stevens

Introduction

Both the early Maori migrants and the later European arrivals had a well developed fishing technology with its associated history and traditions when they came to Aotearoa/New Zealand. Though the new land was quite different to both the Pacific islands and Europe, they soon adapted to its special conditions. They found river mouths and harbours full of fish and shellfish. The Maori used natural materials like flax to make fishing equipment. They made fish traps and nets such as the seine nets, some of which were as long as 1000 metres by 10 metres deep. Line fishing was also an important method of fishing. Fish hooks were made out of bone, wood, stone and shell. Later, when the Maoris came into contact with Europeans, metal was used to fashion hooks, then commercially manufactured fish hooks from Europe replaced the earlier types.

As fish was an important source of food for the Maori people, the small coastal communities often fished together as a unit and divided the catch when they returned home. While the men fished at sea, the women were responsible for collecting shellfish. Surplus fish and shellfish were partially cooked and dried, then stored for consumption during the winter months. Surplus fish was also used for trading with other tribes, particularly inland tribes.

With the arrival of the Europeans, the Maori people traded produce and fish, in some cases supporting the fledgling immigrant communities, until the new arrivals became established. Initially fishermen worked from small open boats propelled by oar or sail. They did not need to venture far offshore as inshore fish stocks were abundant.

Maori fishermen crayfishing at Waipiro Bay on the east coast of the North Island around 1905. (F.A. Hargreaves Collection/Alexander Turnbull Library ref. G2601 1/1)

A fisherman mending his nets with an appreciative audience. The photograph was taken in the north Auckland area at the turn of the century.
(Northwood Collection/ Alexander Turnbull Library ref. G6239 1/1)

With the population base so small, demand was not high and fishing was on a subsistence level, with the majority having to seek other work to subsidise their income from fishing. During these early days there were few regulations and controls, though with the low demand and abundance of large fish the resources were not really threatened. Even if large catches were made there were limited means available to preserve the fish, so catching was followed by immediate consumption, and the fish was sold for a only a small financial return.

These early fishermen mainly used set nets and line fishing to catch fish. By the late 19th century fishing companies were being formed and fishing was becoming a more organised industry. The beginning of the 20th century saw major advances in fishing techniques and technology. Steam and benzine engines had replaced sails and oars. Fishing methods became more efficient and vessels were able to travel further. This new ability to spend more time at sea meant greater productivity and also the ability to explore new fishing grounds. Though the potential catch was greater, statistics for 1914 show that New Zealanders only consumed 2 kg of fish per person a year. A small export market was developed, mainly to Australia where New Zealand smoked fish was highly sought after.

The fishing industry has come a long way since those early pioneer days. Today the industry is highly sophisticated. Technological advances, larger vessels and a highly skilled workforce, both at sea and ashore, have enabled New Zealand's fishing industry to become a world leader.

Research by government and industry groups has added to our knowledge and the introduction of the quota management system has insured that our fishing industry will remain a viable resource for generations to come. Our industry has fortunately been able to learn from other countries' mistakes. Formerly large and healthy fishing industries have now become threatened, and in some cases closed, due to overfishing. These countries now look at New Zealand's system of preserving and enhancing its fish stocks in an attempt to save their own fish resources or rebuild badly depleted numbers.

Another area of importance to the industry is the New Zealand Fishing Industry Board. This organisation was set up in 1963 to represent the interests and to promote the development of the seafood industry. The Fishing Industry Board works closely with government and regional authorities in the decision making process, helping the industry to expand. The board is committed to the principle of making full use of the nation's marine resources on a sustainable basis.

With the development of New Zealand's fishing industry the marketing and promoting of the end product, whether it be fresh, frozen, processed or live, has become a major role of the Fishing Industry Board. The developing and promoting of trade, both here in New Zealand and internationally, in partnership with the industry and other interested parties, is seen as being paramount to the industry's wellbeing. The Fishing Industry Board promotes a greater degree of co-ordination within the seafood industry and also draws the attention of government and the industry to areas where research and development will further enhance the industry.

For many years New Zealand governments basically ignored our fishing industry, choosing instead to focus their attentions on agriculture. This allowed many foreign fishing vessels to reap the benefits of our rich fishing resources, much to the industry's dismay. With the introduction of New Zealand's 200 mile exclusive economic zone (EEZ) in 1979, many of the foreign fishing fleets operating off the New Zealand coast were forced to fish elsewhere or be licenced to fish within the exclusive zone.

With the introduction of the quota management system in 1986, New Zealand took full control of its fisheries resources. This event triggered the rapid development of today's modern progressive seafood industry. As New Zealand's fishing industry grew, many of the vessels licenced to fish in New Zealand waters were also displaced as the industry aimed for complete New Zealandisation. There are still a number of foreign fishing vessels working off the coast but all of these were chartered to catch fish for New Zealand quota holders in the interim.

As mentioned earlier, the Maori people have participated in fishing both commercially and in a recreational form for generations. Today they have a major involvement in New

Maori and European fish processors cleaning yellow eyed mullet, probably for smoking, at the turn of the century. (Northwood Collection/Alexander Turnbull Library ref. G6318 1/1)

Above: Sanford's Fish Market, built in the 1890s in Auckland by Albert Sanford who has been described as the father of Auckland's fishing industry. He was the founder of a company which has become one of the largest fishing companies in New Zealand. (Photograph courtesy of Sanford Ltd)

Below: The auction room at Townsend & Paul Ltd, Wellington, with fish, mainly groper, laid out awaiting auction. (S.C. Smith from D. Davies Collection/Wellington Maritime Museum)

Introduction

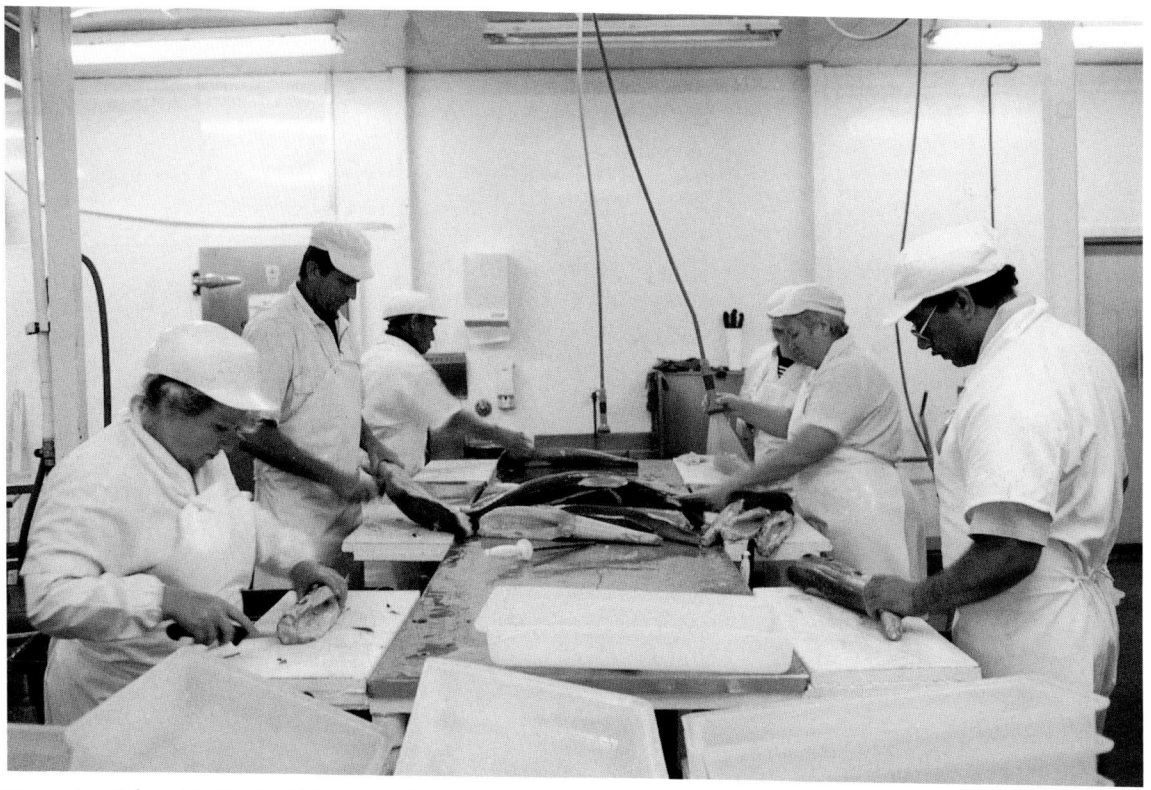

Processing fish inside Fresha Fisheries Ltd's plant in New Plymouth. (Emmanuel Makarios)

Zealand's modern fishing industry. In 1989 the Maori Fisheries Act was passed by government as part of the settlement of the Treaty of Waitangi, signed in 1840. Many Maori groups have been active in expanding their involvement in the industry, buying additional quota and existing fishing ventures. The most significant of these is the establishment of Moana Pacific Fisheries Ltd and the 50% share of Sealord Fisheries Ltd.

Today thousands of people are employed ashore and afloat, and many others not directly involved, such as shopkeepers and truck drivers, airlines and shipping companies, benefit because of New Zealand's fishing industry. Many of these jobs are in the smaller provincial centres such as Bluff, Timaru, Picton, Wanganui, Hawkes Bay, Northland and Nelson, which is New Zealand's largest fishing port.

The fishing industry has now come of age and is proving itself a major player in New Zealand's economy, contributing over one billion dollars a year. With careful planning the industry and New Zealand will continue to grow and prosper. Commercial fishing has developed immensely since those early days when the pioneers in the industry ventured out in their boats to make a living, never thinking that they were laying down the foundations of one of this country's most significant industries.

What follows is a look at some of the people and vessels who represent some of these pioneers.

Chapter One
The *Janie Seddon* and the early years of Talley's Fisheries

In 1925 Ivan Peter Talijancich arrived in New Zealand. Like many who came to this relatively new country, he arrived with plans for a better future. Born in 1908, Ivan came from Igrane in Yugoslavia, and was better known as Ivan Peter Talley.

His first job on arriving in New Zealand was with New Zealand Railways, working on the main trunk line of the North Island, and he saved enough money to open a restaurant in Wellington. Unfortunately this was the time of the Great Depression and many of his customers were unable to pay for their meals.

Ivan Peter Talley, 1908–1964, founder of Talley's Fisheries Ltd. (Courtesy of Talley Fisheries)

Being of a generous nature he was unable to turn these people away. The business eventually failed, mainly because of the economic conditions. This was a setback to his plans, but he had not travelled to the other side of the world just to give up after one attempt and was determined to carry on.

By 1936 Ivan Talley had once again re-established himself, this time in a retail fish business in Motueka. Motueka Fisheries Ltd was situated in High Street, Motueka, on the site of the present fish retail business owned by the Talley family. Though it was initially leased, Ivan Talley purchased the property in 1937.

In August 1938 the Post Office Hotel next to Motueka Fisheries caught fire and was completely destroyed. All that was left standing was the wall between the two buildings. Two days later the wall collapsed onto Ivan Talley's property, demolishing it! This was considered an 'act of God' by the insurance company who refused to pay out for damages. If the wall had collapsed during the fire Ivan Talley would have had full insurance cover.

In 1942 Ivan married Margaret Scott. Margaret was from the lower part of the South Island and had shifted to Motueka in 1939. She was very supportive and hard working, having most of her time taken up in raising a family of four as well as assisting with the establishment of the family business.

Eventually Ivan rebuilt the building and

The *Janie Seddon* undergoing speed trials on the measured mile at Paisley, Scotland. When converted to a trawler its outward appearance changed slightly with the bridge being enclosed and main mast was removed. (Wellington Maritime Museum Collection)

the business. In the redevelopment he built a fish processing area at the rear of the premises. The business started to grow with the construction of a fish factory at Port Motueka on the site of the present factory complex. One of the first major products was fish paste which was manufactured from herrings.

During these early years Ivan Talley relied on local fishing vessels for his fish supply. It was not until 1946 that he purchased the company's first fishing vessel, the *Janie Seddon*. Built in 1901 by Fleming & Ferguson Ltd at Paisley in Scotland, it was intended for the New Zealand Defence Department (Army) for use at Wellington. A vessel of 125 tons, it was 90 feet long, 18 feet wide and had a draft of 9 feet, was powered by two 180 hp steam engines and was twin screw.

Janie Seddon was the first of two submarine minelaying steamers built for service at Wellington and Auckland.

Originally its name was supposed to be "Janie Spotswood" but this was changed in November 1900. The second vessel was called the *Lady Roberts* and they had a similar design. On 28 September 1901 both vessels cleared Greenock and steamed for New Zealand via the Suez Canal, Batavia and Western Australia, arriving at Wellington on 16 January 1902.

The *Janie Seddon* was based at Shelly Bay, Wellington and the *Lady Roberts* at North Head, Auckland. During World War I the *Janie Seddon* operated as an examination vessel. This meant inspecting vessels entering the harbour and looking for anything suspicious, and also ensuring that vessels followed regulations. It is also reported to have laid mines in Wellington Harbour. It was during this time that the *Janie Seddon* was sent to search for a missing scow, the *Southern Isle*, which had last been seen off Farewell Spit. The scow was

Kelly King (left), fisherman, and Ivan Talley aboard the *Janie Seddon* with a bag of fish about to be emptied on the deck. (H. Scott Collection/Wellington Maritime Museum)

eventually found capsized, but without any sign of its crew.

In between the world wars it serviced Somes Island and worked for other Government Departments on Wellington Harbour.

When World War II broke out the *Janie Seddon* was already a military vessel and took up station at Wellington. During the war it served as an examination vessel and liberty boat, and was used for target towing and boom defence work (opening and closing a boom situated inside Wellington Harbour). At the conclusion of World War II it was laid up and offered for sale, having hardly ever ventured beyond the harbour limits in the 45 years it spent in Wellington. It was eventually sold to the Motueka Trawling Co Ltd in December 1946.

Before any fishing could be done the vessel needed some conversion work. This meant removing the crew accommodation in the forward section of the vessel, then insulating and lining this area to act as the fish hold. The coal bunkers were relined with steel, having originally been lined in timber. A large trawl winch was also fitted, which came from an old trawler at Dunedin.

Fishing gear was also installed, with the net being made by "Hocky" who had been a net maker for Sanford Ltd and New Zealand Fisheries Ltd. Ivan Talley had persuaded him to come down to Motueka to make up the nets required for the *Janie Seddon*. He eventually settled in the area and worked from a small shed making and repairing nets for local fishermen. In those days net makers made the nets from scratch and being cotton, were more susceptible to damage, which often happened when the *Janie Seddon* was fishing in an unknown area.

When the alterations were completed the vessel sailed for the fishing grounds under the command of Captain Albert Nalder who had a background in both the merchant navy and the Royal Navy. Initially the *Janie Seddon* fished off the coast of Wanganui. With no depth sounder fishing was quite difficult and on a number of occasions the trawling gear was hooked up on uncharted rocks. The skipper relied mainly on charts but these were not always entirely accurate.

At about the time of the *Janie Seddon*'s purchase, the 17 year old brother of Margaret Talley, Hughie Scott, was visiting Motueka. He had grown up on a dairy farm at Clydevale up the Clutha River near Balclutha in the South Island but was not keen on the farming life. After deciding on a career at sea, he was given a job on the *Janie Seddon* as cook.

His first trip was quite demanding. With the vessel rolling and pitching the galley was not a very nice place to work. During bad weather the galley was often flooded by the

Fish on the deck of the *Janie Seddon* waiting to be gutted and cased. (H. Scott Collection/Wellington Maritime Museum)

sea being shipped aboard. It was not unknown for a sea to wash in one door and out the other. In such conditions it was hard to keep the coal range going! At the end of his first trip Hughie decided he would rather work in the engine room as a fireman and it was decided not to have a full time cook; instead everyone would take turns at cooking.

Work in the engine room was hard on the *Janie Seddon*, Hughie had to shovel coal and grease the engine. He also worked the engine controls when the fishing gear was being deployed or retrieved. The work was much harder than that of the galley but Hughie still preferred it. The chief engineer was Charlie Smith who came from Bluff and had worked on oyster boats before joining the *Janie Seddon*. The chief engineer also shovelled coal; having a small crew, everyone had to pull their weight.

Accommodation aboard the vessel was very good, according to Hughie. The skipper and chief engineer had their own cabins. The crew had their accommodation in the aft cabin, the messroom was on the main deck and the galley was below the wheelhouse.

During the early stages of the fishing venture the *Janie Seddon* fished as far north as Onehunga and down the west coast of the South Island as far as Karamea. Catches of fish were marginal with the vessel being lucky to cover costs. Legislation restricting the areas in which the *Janie Seddon* was allowed to fish seriously affected the venture. Vessels of its size were not permitted to fish within three miles of the coast. This excluded the area of Tasman Bay which was rich in snapper; had it been able to fish in this area, the vessel would have probably done well.

While at Wellington undergoing survey on the patent slip, three new crew members were signed on: they were Fred Blanford, boiler fireman, Bill Dory and Hughie Finlayson, both fishermen. All three were experienced steam trawler crewmen having worked on a number of trawlers out of Wellington. Their knowledge and experience was an asset to the Motueka Trawling Company.

On completing survey the *Janie Seddon* started fishing on the Cape Campbell fishing grounds which were popular with Wellington steam trawlers of the day. Fishing on these grounds was much more productive, though compared to trawlers like the *Maimai*, there was no comparison.

With the fish hold being so far forward trimming the vessel by the stern was difficult when a full load of fish was stowed below. The *Janie Seddon* would trim by the head making steering the vessel difficult. Efforts were made to correct this problem but without very much success. This severely restricted the vessel in the amount of fish it could carry. Another major problem was the length of time it could spend at sea: with only a small coal capacity, it was limited to five days. Extra coal was carried in sacks to give an extra day at sea if required. To reach the fishing ground at Cape Campbell from Motueka took 16 hours which allowed about three days fishing. If fishing was good it could fill up in one day. A full load consisted of 300 cases of fish, not a lot for a vessel of the *Janie Seddon*'s size. The fish caught were mainly tarakihi and hapuka, though sometimes crayfish were trawled up. All fish were gutted prior to being cased and this work was carried out by all crew not engaged on watch.

Prices paid for tarakihi when the *Janie Seddon* was fishing were 2½d a pound. Fisherman working on steam trawlers out of Wellington could earn £100 in a good week's fishing, which was considered very good money when compared with the average pay ashore of £10 a week. But the nature of fishing meant that many trips would be poor. Long hours were spent working, sometimes for days, without a proper break for sleep (this is still the case for many fishermen). On the *Janie Seddon* the hours could vary but generally were not as long as on the larger trawlers.

At different times the *Janie Seddon* would fish off Raglan and in the South Taranaki bight. Sometimes it would call at Castlecliff, Wanganui for coal and stores. Due to regulations of the day the catch could not be sold or discharged in any other port but the vessel's 'home port', which in this case was Motueka. This legislation was seen as a way of protecting fishermen from over-supply of fish in their local markets, thus supposedly ensuring good prices for their catch.

The *Janie Seddon* was also restricted by weather because of its size and design. In bad

Bill Dory (left), fisherman and Hughie Scott, the boiler fireman on the *Janie Seddon*. (H. Scott Collection/ Wellington Maritime Museum)

weather it could not trawl and would have to shelter, while other steam trawlers such as the *Maimai*, being larger and deeper in the water, could continue with their fishing operations.

During its many years of service the *Janie Seddon* had a mainly uneventful life. Its closest brush with disaster was on the night of 8 January 1948. The vessel was homeward bound from fishing near Cape Campbell when it ran aground at Otorohanga Bay where the Cook Strait power cable comes ashore at the North Island.

At the time Hughie Scott had been asleep having come off watch at midnight. When the vessel ran ashore Hughie was thrown from his bunk and woken in a rather startling manner. The skipper initially thought they had collided with another vessel, but was informed on reaching the wheelhouse that the vessel had run aground.

Immediately Wellington Marine Radio was called on an old army radio set which had been converted for marine use and informed of the vessel's plight. At daybreak the skipper and crew inspected the vessel for damage. The bow was high and dry but no serious damage could be found. The crew were put to work transferring cases of fish from the fish hold to the stern of the vessel in an attempt to lighten the bow and settle the vessel by the stern. The Anchor Shipping Company Ltd ferry *Arahura*, hearing of the *Janie Seddon*'s predicament, stood by to offer assistance but was not required and continued on its way.

On closer inspection of the area it was found the *Janie Seddon* had come ashore between two reefs and was extremely lucky!

The *Janie Seddon* on the Patent Slip in Evans Bay, Wellington. (From the W. Signal Estate, Wellington Maritime Museum Collection)

The vessel's lifeboat was used to take a kedge anchor with a wire rope attached out over a nearby reef to be used to haul the vessel back into deep water. At high tide the trawl winch was used to haul on the wire and the main engine was put astern to refloat the vessel. Once afloat the wire was cut and it steamed for Nelson. The salvage operation had been conducted by the skipper and crew without any other assistance which indicated a high level of seamanship by those involved.

On arrival at Nelson it was slipped and inspected by a marine surveyor who found some grazing to the underside of the hull. The *Janie Seddon* was soon fishing again.

On another occasion it was heading for Motueka from fishing off Wanganui and was in the teeth of a northwesterly gale, with a high sea running, and making slow progress. At the same time HMNZS *Black Prince* was in the area. Observing this small ship labouring through the high seas, the commanding officer decided to have a closer look and circled the *Janie Seddon*. The *Janie Seddon*'s skipper, having no concerns about his vessel's abilities in such weather, and being an ex-naval man, felt honoured that the impressive warship should want to view his command and quickly had the New Zealand Ensign run up the mast to salute the warship. On seeing this the HMNZS *Black Prince* turned and continued on her way, satisfied all was well.

As time went by, Ivan Talley realised that the *Janie Seddon* was not at all suited for its role as a trawler and was putting a very serious strain on the Company's finances. In 1948, after only two years of service, it was laid up at the Motueka wharf.

After the *Janie Seddon* was laid up, Hughie Scott continued with his career at sea, working on passenger and cargo ships. He also worked on a number of steam trawlers, eventually buying his own fishing vessels and fishing from Motueka.

Due to a lack of berthage facilities the *Janie Seddon* was shifted to the harbour basin at the port of Nelson, only to be bought back to Motueka a few months later. This time it was anchored in the lagoon and eventually sat on one of its anchors at low tide, damaging its hull and causing the vessel to flood. It was patched up, had all valuables stripped, and was then beached at the Motueka beach frontage near the old Motueka wharf by the Harbour Master, Captain Percy Charles Williams, who was well known in the Nelson area having been a long serving master with the Anchor Shipping Company Ltd.

The remains of the *Janie Seddon* lay where it was beached. Though time has taken its toll, its hull still remains relatively intact.

The *Janie Seddon* venture was a financial failure and caused Ivan Talley considerable difficulty. In 1949 the plant and buildings at the port site had to be sold and were bought by ACE Canning Co Ltd. Ivan Talley had to retrench his business in an attempt to rebuild his company. He once again returned to manage the family fish retail business in the High Street, which had fortunately remained after the episode with *Janie Seddon*.

By 1951 Ivan Talley was once again building up his business which was going from strength to strength. In 1953 the company purchased its first plate freezer and the following year Talley's Fisheries processed a record tonnage of fish, principally for export. The company had reached the point where it could now expand its operations, and in 1955 established a fish processing plant in Nelson under the name of Bay Fisheries Ltd. The following year was a very significant one in that the fish factory at Port Motueka was repurchased from ACE Canning Co Ltd. From this point the

Above: The *Janie Seddon* as it appears today on the foreshore at Motueka. (E. Makarios/Wellington Maritime Museum Collection)

Left: 'Hockey' the net maker who Ivan Talley persuaded to come to Motueka to make the nets required for his vessel. (H. Scott Collection/Wellington Maritime Museum Collection)

company shifted its processing operations back to Motueka. New lines of fresh and prepared seafood products were developed and expanded. In 1963 Ivan's eldest sons entered the family business, ensuring continued family control of it.

In 1964 Ivan Peter Talley died. His perseverance, determination and foresight through good times and bad, had laid the foundations of a company which in a relatively short time has become one of New Zealand's premiere fishing companies. On his death his family took over the reins of the business and have expanded and steered it through major developments in New Zealand's fishing industry.

Though the *Janie Seddon* was a failure as a fishing vessel, valuable lessons were learnt by Ivan Talley and his family which only strengthened their resolve to succeed.

References

R.J. McDougall, *New Zealand Naval Vessels*, GP Books, 1989

A. Scott, *Talley's Fisheries Ltd of Motueka, the first 50 years*

Acknowledgements

Hughie Scott
Peter Talley
Stuart Dixon

Chapter Two

Pioneer fishermen of Island Bay

Situated on Wellington's south coast is a place of rugged beauty; on a hot, calm summer's day it can resemble a sleepy little fishing village in the Mediterranean, yet on a day when the wind is howling from the south the resemblance is instead more to the coast of northern Scotland. This place is Island Bay, now one of Wellington's most populated suburbs. Originally, however, it was not considered suitable for human habitation but was only a picnic destination; and even then only when the weather was favourable. In its early days the 'bay' was fairly bleak, windswept and marshy, particularly on the floor of the valley (which the Parade, the suburb's main thoroughfare now occupies) as a stream ran through it to the sea.

The Italians

During those early years around the turn of the century, Island Bay's main inhabitants were fishermen who lived in small huts on the foreshore and worked their small double-ended open boats around the island and along the coast, setting their nets. These men were mainly Italians and Shetland Islanders. The first Italians to settle in Wellington lived in Eastbourne, most of whom came from Massalubrense in the Bay of Naples and Stromboli, an island to the northwest of Sicily.

A panoramic view of fishing boats at their moorings in 1931, showing Taputeranga Island which the locality takes its name from. On visiting the 'bay' today, it is difficult to imagine so many boats moored there. (Wellington Maritime Museum)

These people had been fishermen or worked on the land back in their homeland. Many of the Italians who settled in Wellington chose to fish for a living, working their boats on Wellington Harbour and its entrance. When the weather was suitable, they would venture beyond the harbour entrance to catch warehou. Many families settled in Eastbourne, and names such as Russo, Dellabarca, Meo and Basile were and are still common in the area.

By the early 1920s many of the fishermen based at Eastbourne chose to work their boats from Island Bay instead, for, by then, the suburb had begun to grow and develop. The boats were now bigger and this new location gave them more protection from the elements.

Besides the Italians, there were Scots from the north of Scotland and Shetland Islanders working in the bay. They were a rugged lot, used to working the tempestuous sea around the shores of their homeland. Their experience of seas governed by strong tides and rips prepared them well for fishing in Cook Strait.

And the Shetland Islanders

The shift by many of the Eastbourne fishermen and the settlement of Shetland Islanders at the 'bay' was mainly due to its proximity to the fishing grounds. Island Bay offered better protection from the prevailing northwest wind and in southerly winds offered limited protection to the fishing vessels moored there, depending on the severity of the conditions. Initially the boats moored near the island for better protection, but by the 1930s overcrowding forced some boats to moor near the beach, which is much more exposed to southerly storms. At this time the boats were usually owned by two or more partners. It was only later as some of the fishermen became more prosperous that they began owning their boats outright.

One of the early Shetland Islanders to settle in Island Bay was William Bruce. In a letter written to his grandfather, dated 15 June 1922, he tells of a 34-foot boat called *Lerwick* which he and Magnus Arthur bought together. He describes the types of fish caught in this part of the world compared to

Early fishermen's huts on the western side of Island Bay near Fishermen's Creek. Note that the nets have been flaked out to dry. The photograph was taken around 1900. (Alexander Turnbull Library Collection, ref G36457)

the Shetland Islands. In a letter to his father later in the same year he writes about the poor prices paid to fishermen and gives an example of threepence per pound for groper, complaining that the same fish is sold in the shop for tenpence per pound. He goes on to tell his father of the main species of fish caught by the Island Bay fishermen – groper, hake, ling and shark. He gives the average weight for the first three as twenty, nine and eighteen pounds. William concludes by telling his father that there are about 25 Shetland Islanders in Wellington and they have set up the Shetland Society to organise a few social gatherings for their community.

Both the Shetland Island and Italian communities were very close knit. They rarely socialised together but co-existed well, and if one of the fishing community got into difficulties they would all rally to help the best they could.

Two fishermen who were eventually to settle in Island Bay were Santo Saffioti and Jimmy Imlach, Snr. Santo arrived in New Zealand in 1912 aboard an Italian naval training vessel from which he jumped ship in Auckland, eventually making his way to Wellington. At first he fished from Eastbourne, then later he settled in Island Bay and fished from there. Jimmy came to New Zealand after the first World War, working at a timber mill, then aboard a coastal vessel before settling in Island Bay. Both married and had families, and in the early 1930s both their sons, Paolo and Jimmy, Jnr, followed in their fathers' footsteps to become fishermen. Paolo went fishing with Santo on his boat, the *All Black*; while Jimmy went fishing with his father on the *Southern Cross*, owned by Tommy Isbister, a Shetland Islander. This was a typical scenario for most of the fishermen's sons at the 'bay' and probably most fishing communities around New Zealand.

Both boys had chosen a bad time to enter the workforce as the country was in the grip of the Great Depression. Many of the boats at

Island Bay were forced to reduce their crews. Jimmy was one of the unfortunate ones and had to leave the *Southern Cross*, but it did not take him long to find another boat.

The Depression

Like the rest of New Zealand, the Island Bay fishing community was severely affected by the 1930s Depression. The fishermen were having difficulty selling their fish as wholesalers were offering lower prices, and occasionally refusing to buy fish due to oversupply. It was not unknown for fishermen to take the catch back out to sea and dump it; wholesalers charged others for dumping their fish. Sometimes fishermen preferred to take their fish to the Home of Compassion in Island Bay or to an orphanage in the nearby suburb of Berhampore.

Before the Depression fishermen had made a reasonable living, but with the Depression it became a subsistence living, with many fishing to feed themselves and waiting for things to improve. Life became so desperate for the fishing community that the fishermen of Island Bay and Eastbourne called a meeting to discuss their futures. The meeting was held at a hall in Eastbourne owned by Antonio Dellabarca and was attended by approximately 70 fishermen from both communities. At the meeting they decided to establish the Wellington Fishermen's Co-operative Ltd. This was a most significant event for the fishermen and their families. Some of the foundation members were Alex Wilson, Tony Basile, Santo Saffioti, Antonio Dellabarca, Battiste Meo,

Early fishermen at Island Bay about 1900. (Alexander Turnbull Library Collection, ref. 56420)

Jack Tait hauls a groper aboard the *San Marco*. (D. Davies Collection/Wellington Maritime Museum)

Jack, Peter and Andrew Tait. These people were the main driving force in convincing their colleagues that the formation of a co-operative was in their interest.

The Wellington Fishermen's Co-operative

Salvi Dellabarca, the son of Antonio, liaised between the Co-op and solicitors to ensure all the correct paperwork was in place and a constitution was drawn up. Each member of the Co-operative was issued with 40 shares. To build up some capital each member paid £5 (equal to five shares) back to the Co-op. Premises had to be found, and Alec Wilson, Jack Tait and Antonio Dellabarca met with representatives of the Wellington City Council to discuss the venture and suitable premises. They arranged for the Co-op to occupy the old municipal milk department building at 75 Dixon Street, in the heart of the city, a site now occupied by Deka. The building was particularly suitable as it had refrigeration and concrete floors. During World War II the Co-op purchased the building, eventually selling out in 1963.

Initially members of the Co-op were guaranteed a minimum of 25 shillings per week. This sum was a very basic retainer and comparable to the unemployment benefit of later years. Before the setting up of the Co-op fishermen had no guaranteed income, so the retainer ensured they would not go hungry during this difficult period. Once the Co-op built up its customer base and finances, members received the normal going rate. In its early years the Co-op also owned three fish retail shops in the city that were managed for the Co-op.

TELEGRAMS & CABLES "HAPUKA" TELEPHONES 50-437 & 51-194

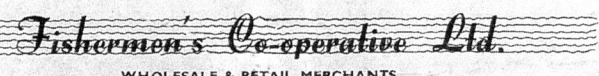

Fishermen's Co-operative Ltd.

WHOLESALE & RETAIL MERCHANTS
FISH, CRAYFISH, OYSTERS & RABBITS Etc.

•

75 DIXON STREET,
WELLINGTON, C.1

They appointed eight directors, all skippers, of whom two were expected to stand down each year for the following four years. On standing down each could stand for re-election if they chose. Eventually the Co-op's directors consisted of both skippers and crew. A Mr Kane was appointed as manager, a position he held from 1930-36. His successors were Bill Connor, 1936-45, Gordon Morrison 1945-54, and Salvi Dellabarca from 1954 until the demise of the Co-op in 1963.

The Co-op was set up with two departments: one was for filleting and fish preparation for retailers, and later government contracts; the other for smoking, by the late 1940s they were smoking thirty 60-pound boxes of fish per day. They generally smoked blue cod, ling and warehou.

Government contracts consisted of supplying fish to hostels, prisons, and army and airforce bases in Wellington. These contracts were tendered for each year and the Wellington Fishermen's Co-operative tendered successfully for several years. To be more competitive, the fish sold by the Co-op was slightly cheaper than other wholesalers. In its day the Co-op employed fifteen people and sold fish as far north as Cambridge, becoming one of New Zealand's leading fish wholesalers.

The Co-op initially operated 28 boats, a substantial number for any organisation of its type. After the war the Co-op offered its members interest-free loans for the purchase of new engines and fishing gear, and major refits. Profits were divided equally between the membership and in a good year of trading

Tom Isbister (left) and another crewman gutting groper aboard the *River Nile* around 1930. (D. Davies Collection/ Wellington Maritime Museum)

members were also paid bonuses.

After 33 years as one of the country's main fish wholesalers and exporters, problems within the membership of the Co-op caused a rift that could not be resolved. They sold the building to Woolworths for £40,000 and other assets were sold to various fishing companies. In its time the Co-op was very successful and gave its members a comfortable and secure living. It ceased to exist in 1963.

Fishing grounds

As Island Bay was situated near the main fishing grounds of the 1920s, it only took about an hour to get to the nearest of the fishing banks. They fished in depths of 60, 120, 220 and 300 fathoms. Many fishing areas were named, for example, Fouler Bank, Napoli Bank, Middle Bank and Island Bay Bank. These were often named after the boat or person who found it or after a nearby landmark.

The main methods of catching fish were line fishing, nets and craypots. In those early days the demand for crayfish was not high and those fishermen using set nets for butterfish, moki and warehou saw crayfish caught in the nets as a nuisance rather than a windfall.

Technology

During the early stages of the fishing industry's development fishing boats at Island Bay were basic and unsophisticated, and used oars and sails to manoeuvre. Later, with bigger boats built, first benzine and later diesel engines were fitted.

There were several competent boatbuilders among the fishing communities of Eastbourne and Island Bay. Some specialised in building the double-ended carvel dinghies used by the fishermen to get to and from the boats on their moorings. They were also used to set nets to catch sardines and mackerel for bait. Before boats were fitted with winches, the fishermen hauled up the groper lines and crayfish pots by hand. It is believed that the first boat fitted with a winch at Island Bay was the *River Nile,* owned by Shetland Islander

Frank Dellabarca (left) and Jack Imlach unload their dinghy after a day on the fishing grounds. (P. Saffioti Collection/Wellington Maritime Museum)

A good catch of groper being hauled aboard the River Nile *in Cook Strait. (Wellington Maritime Museum collection)*

Jack Tait. The winch was made from the rear axle and differential of a motor vehicle and it seems to have been very temperamental.

Engineer Norman Jack built and fitted winches to many of the Island Bay boats. The winches made life easier, as they no longer had the backbreaking work of pulling in lines by hand, however, it also brought the risk of being caught up in the winch and seriously injured. In those early days several accidents occurred. On one occasion an Italian fisherman, who operated his vessel single handed, was hauling in one of his crayfish pots when he was caught around the leg by the winch. Unable to free himself he had to hop around the capstan drum until the crayfish pot jammed up against the block. The fisherman received serious leg injuries but recovered to fish again.

On another occasion one of the large boats was returning from a day's groper fishing. On this particular day the drum end of the winch would not stop turning unless a rope was placed around it and secured to some part of the boat, in this case the skipper chose to secure it around the cabin. Unknown to the skipper, the vibration of the engine eased the strain on the rope which in turn allowed the winch to start revolving. Suddenly the top of the wheelhouse was torn off! Fortunately no one was injured. But this new technology certainly took some getting used to.

Equipment

The fishing community was not just made up of fishermen, for the women also played a part by making fishing gear and equipment. It was the women who made the oilskin smocks worn by the fishermen. Oilskins could be bought readymade, but most fishermen preferred the homemade version as they were more pliable and easier to work in. The smocks were made of Japara cloth on the outside and light calico cloth on the inside. Once the smock was made, it was then oiled with linseed oil and hung outside to allow the oil to soak in and dry, which could take days or weeks. Then it was worn for a few days to allow it to harden with the salt spray. Then it was once again oiled and hung to dry before normal use. Most fishermen had two as they were not entirely waterproof. When they became wet they would become heavy and unpleasant to work in. Many a fisherman must have shuddered at the thought of having to put on a wet oilskin in the early hours of a winter's morning!

As most of the fishing boats working from Island Bay from 1920 to the 1950s were involved in line fishing, an important part of their equipment was the buoys used with the fishing lines. Initially the fishermen used barrels or fuel drums, but as Cook Strait has very strong tidal currents, at times the floats would be swept underwater and could not be retrieved until the tide slackened. Due to the water pressure, many of these makeshift buoys would implode and the fishing gear would be lost. The Shetland Islanders introduced buoys made of canvas. They cut out six panels, using a pattern, and then sewed them together, though with great difficulty. There were two versions of these buoys, one was fitted with a stick through it like a danbuoy, and the other was fitted with an eye to which the line was attached. The canvas was sewn together and finally tied around a wooden plug which had a hole in it so the buoy could be inflated. Generally, the women of the community did this work.

Each buoy was oiled inside and out using linseed oil and then painted with red lead to make them waterproof. To get paint into the seams inside the buoy the paint had to be blown in by some unfortunate person to make sure it got into all the nooks and crannies. Tar was also used to make them waterproof. Each morning, before the buoys were used, one of the crew, preferably the boy, if one was carried, had to blow them up!

Floats used to mark crayfish pots and set nets were normally made of tarred cork. Often the Island Bay fishermen would go to the Patent Slip in Evans Bay, Wellington, to see if they could buy any old cork lifebuoys condemned off the ships surveyed there. They cut the lifebuoys to the appropriate size for use as marker buoys. If lifebuoys were not available, sheets of cork were purchased and cut up. The cork floats used on the headline of their nets were also cut and drilled by the fishermen.

Crayfish

Crayfish was not in great demand during the early years with the only market being the local one. Crayfish was sold on the beach and sometimes pre-cooked. Before refrigeration triangular holding pots were moored at Island Bay and were used to keep the crayfish alive until they were required. In the best part of the season three holding pots were moored in the 'bay'. Boats crayfishing during the 1920s-1930s used only 10-15 crayfish pots as crayfish were so abundant. If it was a good season some fish wholesalers would put limits on the amount of crayfish that could be landed. If too much was landed, and it could not be sold, it would be carted to the dump. In those days there were no restrictions on size, but the abundance of large crayfish meant there was no need for size restrictions as the fishermen had no difficulty in getting good sized fish.

Sometimes in a bad southerly a holding pot would come ashore and there would be crayfish scattered along the beach with members of the public helping themselves to a feed of crayfish. The fishermen were not at all bothered about this: in fact, if someone wanted a crayfish they were told to help themselves out of the holding pot.

During the mid 1950s Salvi and Joe Dellabarca went over to the Wairarapa coast to make a commercial assessment regarding the catching of crayfish on that coast. It was at this time that an agency was set up to export New Zealand crayfish to the United States and the Co-op was examining a

A view of the Island Bay fishing fleet taken during the 1950s. (Wellington Maritime Museum Collection)

number of possibilities to enable its members to take advantage of this new market.

About this time Frank Dellabarca, who was fishing from Island Bay, did an exploratory crayfishing trip to Cape Palliser. Using ring pots (a ring 3-4 feet across with netting attached to it) he managed to catch over one hundred 110-pound sacks of crayfish in a day's fishing! Some 15-20 pots were set in a line and left for a short time, then hauled and cleared, reset and the procedure repeated.

Frank's return to Island Bay caused a great deal of interest and over the following weeks many of the Co-op fishermen made or bought ring pots to take advantage of this market. As mentioned earlier, crayfish were plentiful off the coast of Island Bay, but the numbers caught during the mid to late 1950s were exceptional for the area.

On one occasion the Co-op was inundated with over 1,000 110-pound sacks of crayfish, far too much for the normal staff to cope with, and they called in fishermen to help with the processing. In its first year of exporting crayfish the Co-op exported 11,000 cartons.

The Bait Boat

During the 1930s a Mr Deacon from Port Underwood would bring his boat over to Island Bay loaded with mackerel to sell to the fishermen as bait. Most of the fishermen would buy from him. Sometimes he would bring over up to 800 cases with many buying 80 cases and freezing them to use as groper bait. When not using mackerel they would use barracouta. Later they used to go to the Marlborough Sounds to catch sardines for bait. During World War II there was a

Anyone who has worked in Cook Strait will know how temperamental the weather conditions can be. Here a fishing boat heads back to Island Bay after being caught in a southerly gale. (Wellington Maritime Museum)

sardine factory in Picton, owned by Brown & Barretts Ltd, canning fish for export. In that time a few of the Island Bay fishermen worked in the Sounds catching sardines for the factory.

World War II

Official attitudes during World War II caused a great deal of ill feeling and bitterness among the Italian community at Island Bay, as many of their people were interned as enemy aliens. This caused a great deal of anguish and hardship for the wives and children of those fishermen interned on Somes Island in Wellington Harbour. The authorities felt that every precaution should be taken to ensure national security. Initially, they considered prohibiting Italians from fishing but decided against this as it may have made the supply of fish difficult and would have left the fishermen unemployed, which could have led to further problems. By the middle of 1940 they had decided that Italians could fish but they needed police permission and had to allow their vessels and gear to be inspected.

Several of these inspection points were set up around the North Island, including Island Bay. Boats were inspected before leaving for the fishing grounds and on their return. Because Island Bay was the inspection point for the Wellington region any Italian boats at Makara and Eastbourne had to shift to Island Bay to enable them to fish. Boats were restricted as to where they could go and they had to be in by sunset. The skippers had to keep a daily log and the cabin tops were painted red for easy identification by the shore stations, inspection vessels and aircraft.

Maintenance

Maintenance is a never-ending problem with any vessel and was even more so during the pioneer years of the Island Bay fishing fleet. Much of the maintenance was done by the crews; among them were a few who were knowledgeable about engines and boat building. Slipping facilities were non-existent, so the larger vessels were taken into

Wellington to be slipped at B.J.L. Jukes' boatyard at Balaena Bay. Smaller boats were beached in Fishermen's Creek on the western side of the 'bay' or Joe Boom Creek on the eastern side of the 'bay' near the Esplanade. Joe 'Boom' Greco was an early Italian arrival at Island Bay and was a fisherman there for many years, owning a number of boats which were often beached for maintenance on that part of the beach. Boats as long as 40 feet were hauled up using a block and tackle hauled by the fish truck. As many as 30 fishermen would help by keeping the boat upright while it was being hauled out.

During World War II Mr C.B. Cunningham, a marine engineer, built a slipway in Fishermen's Creek. The area had originally been surveyed by the Wellington City Council and a design drawn up for a slipway. Eventually they handed the proposal over to Cunningham who, in 1941, built a small slipway and erected a 40-foot high gantry for lifting heavy equipment on or off vessels using the slip. Due to the war, work on the slip ceased, recommencing after the war's end. In 1955 Cunningham began work to increase the size of the slipway. The rocky sea floor was gelignited in preparation for a 300-foot graded slipway track.

Initially the fishermen used the slip, as it saved them a trip into Wellington or other ports for maintenance. But, due to the lack of facilities, the Island Bay fishermen returned to using the slipping facilities in Wellington, Picton or Nelson. The slipway eventually closed due to lack of use, and all that remained to remind people of its existence was the gantry which stood over the slipway. The gentle slope created for the slipway was used by some of the smaller boats for beaching and painting until recent years. During the 1970s a large trailer and tractor were used to haul out some of the smaller boats for painting and other maintenance. Fishing vessels based at Island Bay now use slipping facilities at Wellington or travel to other ports for maintenance.

After the war the Fishermen's Co-op, represented by Salvi Dellabarca, negotiated with the Wellington City Council for the construction of a bait shed, which was built on the foreshore. At the one end of the shed were several lockers that were allocated to the fishermen for storage. Salvi also arranged with Caltex New Zealand for a diesel pump and tank to be placed on the foreshore near the bait shed to provide fuel for the Co-op's fishing fleet.

Over the years there have been a number of proposals to build a breakwater and jetty facilities at Island Bay to enable the fishing fleet to be better serviced, none of which have eventuated.

The Wholesale Business

Both the Italian and Shetland Island communities at Island Bay included budding entrepreneurs who got involved in the shoreside operations of the fishing industry. Names such as Tony Paino, Vincenzo Barnao, Peter Isbister, and Albert and Lib Meo come to mind, each of whom, in their time, were among the major fish wholesalers in Wellington.

Tony Paino had come to New Zealand in 1900 as a boy. As a teenager he owned a horse and cart and set up a business carting fish from Makara to the market. But the business failed and he got work with the New Zealand Trawling Company. After owning a number of fish businesses in Masterton and Palmerston North, he then purchased the fish business owned by a Greek, N. Fernando, later buying Hawke's Bay Fisheries, which was based in Wellington. After World War II

Groper lines being hauled aboard the *River Nile*. It is believed to have been the first vessel at Island Bay to be fitted with a winch. (D. Davies Collection/Wellington Maritime Museum)

he amalgamated with the New Zealand Trawling Company to become New Zealand Fisheries. His partners in the venture were Vincenzo Barnao and Bradstock and Willy. They also owned several fish retail shops around the city.

Other Italians from Island Bay owned fish retail ships. Some had been fishermen but found the hours and work in fish retail more appealing than working in Cook Strait in the middle of winter.

The Shetland community also had one of its sons in the fish wholesale business. Peter Isbister was born in Lerwick in the Shetland Islands. He came out to New Zealand in 1912 when he shipped out as 3rd mate on the Union Steam Ship Company's cargo vessel *Wairuna*, on which he was captured by the German raider *Wolf* during World War I. After his release he eventually made his way back to New Zealand and bought a grocery store in Johnsonville, one of Wellington's northern suburbs. Some time later he sold the store and shifted to Island Bay where he established Cook Strait Fisheries Ltd.

The premises of Cook Strait Fisheries were on the Parade in the main shopping centre of Island Bay. Eventually, they owned several vessels, as well as the fish retail shop at the front of the premises. The building and shop still exist with the shop now called Parade Fisheries Ltd.

Today

The Island Bay fishing fleet has shrunk since its heyday, when there were over 30 fishing boats moored in the bay. Now there are only 6 to 10 boats working from there. Some boats that moored there previously now use the main wharves or the marinas in Wellington Harbour, where it is safer and more convenient for fishermen to service their boats.

The boats have, of course, changed since those early days, and today a round bilge displacement vessel is rarely seen in the bay. The majority are now hard chine, semi-planing or planing vessels. No longer do the majority of the crews and skippers have Italian or Shetland Island names. Most of the sons and grandsons of the pioneers have chosen easier ways to make a living. Though Italians are still very much involved in the fishing industry, they now tend to be more involved in the wholesale and export side of the business. Some now own large trawlers and longliners which are fishing both within and outside New Zealand's exclusive economic zone. But their numbers are few compared to those early years.

In years gone by, fishermen young and old would gather at the wall along Island Bay beach, talking about how it used to be in the 'good old days' and having a good laugh. Sadly, there are only a few pioneers left now to pass on their memories.

References

Paul Elenio, *Alla Fine Del Mondo, To the Ends of the Earth*

Acknowledgements

My sincere thanks to Paolo Saffioti and the late Jimmy Imlach for allowing me to interview them. My thanks also to Lib Dellabarca who I interviewed regarding the Wellington Fishermen's Co-operative. Lib was one of the Directors and the last Sales Manager for the Co-op.

The Island Bay Fishermen's football team of 1921 was made up of both Italians and Shetland Islanders. (Alexander Turnbull Library Collection, ref F56701)

Chapter Three
The early fishermen of Paremata's Hobson Street remembered

On the lower west coast of the North Island of New Zealand is the harbour of Porirua, and on its shore is the suburb of Paremata. This area has a long history of Maori settlement, shore whaling, farming and fishing. Porirua harbour and its surrounding hills had an abundance of food which made the area ideal for settlement, firstly by the Maori and then by the pakeha.

The first regular contact between Maori and pakeha took place about 1820 as sealers and flax traders were working around Cook Strait. Later a number of shore whaling stations were established along the coast; one was established at the entrance to Porirua harbour in 1835 and was known as Parramatta. This station was run by Joseph Toms and at its peak operated seven whale boats and employed 40 men, among whom were Paremata's first Pakeha residents.

One of the early Pakeha settlers to work from the area as a fisherman was John May, who had travelled out to New Zealand with his wife and six children from the north east of Scotland in 1886. In Scotland, John May and other members of his family had been fishermen, fish curers, fish smokers, coopers (barrel makers) and crofters. Skilled in catching fish (mainly herrings), they cured and pickled the fish and barrelled them ready for the market. At the time the herring fishery in Britain and Europe was huge and, in fact, was the first large scale commercial fishery in the western world as it had been started by the Dutch in the 16th century.

When John May arrived in New Zealand he first purchased land for farming at Glenside, near Johnsonville, but the lure of the sea was too strong and he went fishing as well. With the assistance of his son, John Alec May, and his son-in-law, Thomson Bruce, who had worked for John May back in Peterhead, Scotland, he set up a fishing business in Paremata. They built fish curing sheds, a smokehouse and cooperage along the foreshore of Paremata. They purchased a

John May as he appeared in his later years. (Henderson family collection)

A view of some of the Paremata fishing fleet with what was to be known as Hobson Street in the background, about 1900. (Henderson family collection)

boat, employed a number of men to fish and work in the sheds and they themselves fished. Other fishermen in the area also supplied them with fish.

The operation was small and unsophisticated by today's standards, but at the time was considered to be high tech. The Mays and others introduced technology and skills to the Paremata area from the other side of the world.

As time passed other fishermen settled in the area, many of whom had only recently arrived in New Zealand. These people settled along the foreshore, building small baches on the inter-tidal zone, which made living there precarious when gale force conditions blew in from the west. Even at high tide the water lapped the floorboards and during spring tides some of the baches flooded, which made life difficult and uncomfortable.

By 1900 John May was an old man; the Mays sold their farm and left the fishing industry. They settled in Johnsonville, John Alec May opening a grocery store in the area. John May's son-in-law, Thomson Bruce, continued to fish and ran the shore operation until the mid 1930s.

Another early fisherman at Paremata was Joe Foster, who is believed to have first gone to sea as a boy of 14. Though he was unable to read and write, he was a skilled fisherman. This was not uncommon among fishermen at the time. Other names from those early days of fishing at Paremata are Vella, whose family farmed nearby Mana Island for many years, McKenzie, Pegani, Gestro, Lima, Barry, Lambert, Buckland and Johnson.

Fishing, of course, was done inshore, with many of the boats being single handed or with a skipper and deckhand. Boats were small, with most being about 20 feet in length. Fishing methods consisted of hand-lining,

A view of Hobson Street, looking south towards the station. The close proximity to the sea and railway line is plainly evident. A northbound AB-hauled express is about to cross the Paremata bridge. (Porirua Museum collection)

long lining, set nets, drag nets and crayfishing using supplejack pots.

It was during the early 1900s that the grandson of John May, Jim Henderson, started to spend his weekends and spare time among the fishing community of Paremata. Fishing was a fascination for Jim Henderson and he had no better tutors than those fishermen.

His father, Captain John Henderson, was a harbour pilot at Wellington, based at Worser Bay, near the entrance to the port. With the outbreak of World War I Jim Henderson enlisted in the army and served overseas, where he was captured and put in a prisoner of war camp. At the end of the war he returned to New Zealand and went commercial fishing with his uncle, Thomson Bruce, who in 1916 had bought the famous Bailey-built racing yacht, the *Pet*, from Wellington. After some conversion work and the installation of a Frisco Standard benzine engine, it joined the growing fishing fleet at Paremata. Both men worked the *Pet* as far south as Makara or Warehou Bay, as it was known among the fishing communities, and as far north as Kapiti Island.

In those days fishermen did not have to travel far as fish were abundant. Often these men would overnight at Makara with other fishermen. Social evenings were held ashore with the local fishing community, smoking and having a quiet drink, talking about the weather and the day's catch. The Makara fishing community was mainly made up of Italian fishermen, one of whom, Joe (Giuseppe) Volpicelli, lived to the age of 101, spending most of those years as a fisherman at Makara. Another well known fisherman in those early years was Victor Leopold Haupois, otherwise known as French Louis, who arrived from France and settled in Makara in 1875.

During those years the main fish species targeted were groper, blue cod, butterfish, snapper and warehou. During the 1920s and 1930s large catches of warehou were made by the Paremata fishermen. It was not unusual for a fishing boat to come in with a thousand warehou, most of which was smoked as refrigeration was not common. A popular area for catching warehou was near Mana Island, the area was known as the 'warehou set' where hundreds of yards of nets were set.

On one occasion a boat called the *Thistle* was returning from the warehou set with approximately 700 warehou aboard, so deeply laden that its exhaust began taking water, which stalled the engine and forced the crew to row home. A vessel not so lucky was the fishing boat *Matakitaki*, owned by Henry and Alexander Brown. In August 1928 they had gone out to Mana Island to retrieve their warehou nets when they were caught in a fierce northerly gale. The vessel capsized on the bar at the entrance to Porirua Harbour with the loss of its two man crew, one of the few occasions that fishermen lost their lives crossing this bar.

The area the fishermen lived in on the foreshore was unofficially given the name Hobson Street in the 1920s by a group of locals who had been celebrating. The story goes that they took down the sign at Hobson Street in Wellington, which was in a well-to-do part of the city and nailed it to a lamp post

Fishermen pose with a good day's catch made up of butterfish, moki, snapper, groper and ling. From left: Henry Brown, Alexander McKenzie, Ronald Brown (later Reverend Brown) and Alexander Brown. Henry and Alexander Brown drowned on 23 August 1928 when the *Matakitaki* capsized. (Porirua Museum collection)

Jim Henderson sits on the beach having his lunch after setting his nets. This was a common practice as the small launches could be anchored in the shallows. (Henderson family collection)

at Paremata. From then on it was known as Hobson Street by the locals, rather than the derogatory names used previously, such as slum alley or slug alley. Eventually, in 1948, the name became official.

The fishermen and their families who inhabited these baches were a humble, yet proud group of people, unsophisticated, who took life on the chin. Their lives were made even more difficult with the Great Depression in the 1930s. Most of the fish caught at that time was sold to fish wholesalers in Wellington and had to be sent into town by train. During the Depression it was common for a fisherman to be charged more for transporting his fish to town than he earned from his catch. This happened to Joe Foster who found it hard to understand, but being used to life's hard knocks he just shrugged and decided to catch fish only to eat, until things got better or he could find a local market for his catch.

One of the more productive times of year from a fishing point of view was February-March when large shoals of snapper would gather off the coast. The fishermen would go up to Kapiti Island and then drift south back towards Porirua harbour, hand lining for snapper. They would return home with chaff sacks full of fish. Before the Depression they had made a good living at this time of year, but in those desperate times they were lucky to receive one shilling per chaff sack of cleaned snapper. The fishermen of Hobson Street barely eked out a living at this time. They would not have survived, had they not built their baches on the foreshore on land which belonged to New Zealand Railways or the Marine Department, as the rent was a nominal charge of one pound per year. The main drawback of living where they did was that at any time they could be served with notice which required them to move off the land.

By the time of the Depression another generation of Hendersons were spending their weekends and school holidays among the fishing community of Hobson Street. John and Murray were the sons of Jim Henderson who had fished with Thomson Bruce aboard the *Pet*. Jim had left fishing during the mid 1920s and returned to his trade as a printer but continued to spend much of his spare time with his wife and

Hobson Street fishermen, a hardy yet humble group. Standing from left: Thomson Bruce, rest unknown; sitting: Joe Foster, Ted Barry (with accordion), Joe Pegani. (Porirua Museum collection)

children at their bach at Hobson Street. Like their father, John and Murray were deeply fascinated with fishing and the area.

They recall as boys walking into a bach owned by a fisherman, George Peters, which was like going back 100 years. Life was very basic and these early fishermen did not have high expectations. Some of the fishermen were quite religious, others were superstitious. John and Murray felt these fishermen had integrity, and that the local community trusted these men and held them in high regard, even though they were shabbily dressed and lived in poor conditions. The fishermen had their own code of ethics and anyone who broke their rules was literally run out of town. Living in these less than perfect conditions made these people hard. Not many complained of sickness, charity was not easily accepted, and if someone did assist any of the fishing community, they would receive a bundle of fish in return.

An example of the endurance of these men is a series of accidents that befell Jimmy Andrews. Jimmy had been chopping firewood when a splinter flew up into his eye and dislodged it. He pushed the eye back in and calmly walked along the railway line to Porirua Hospital for medical assistance. Jimmy's second accident occurred while the road bridge was being built at Paremata. He had been sitting on the edge of the railway line talking to the workmen and did not hear the train approaching around the corner. He was struck by the cow catcher and received serious injuries to one side of his body. The impact threw him over the side of the bridge, but managing to hold on, he was eventually rescued by a work punt. An ambulance was called and he was made comfortable in a wicker chair and given a packet of cigarettes as it took the ambulance 35 minutes to arrive from Wellington. Not only was Jimmy hardy, he seems to have been accident prone!

By the 1940s the early fishermen that John and Murray remember were old men. New boats and men were now working out of Paremata. Diesel engines were replacing benzine engines. John Henderson remembers the local petrol station, owned by Doug Bruce, having a pump at the front of the station marked 'launch spirit'. This was low grade petrol which was not suitable for motor vehicles as it was a lower octane. This was just as well as, according to John, many of the fishermen he knew were not too careful where they threw their fag ends, with many actually ending up in the bilge of the boat which had a mixture of fuel and water in it. Doug Bruce did a lot of engineering for the fishermen, fitting propeller shafts and repairing engines.

As boys John and Murray would often help the fishermen with their drag nets which they used inside Porirua harbour to catch flounders and bait. They would also go out fishing on some of the local boats; an extra person on board was usually welcomed as it meant that an extra hand line could be used. It was while on holiday from school that John Henderson went out fishing with Joe Foster on his boat, the *Wee Elsie*. They had just recovered their nets when the engine stalled. Joe immediately began to tinker with the engine in an attempt to restart it, at the same time talking away and gesturing to it. John, thinking that he was speaking to him, was sharply informed that Joe was not talking to him but to the engine!

On another occasion John had gone fishing with Joe and having laid their nets, they went to anchor to have some lunch. John was about to take a bite out of his sandwich when Joe enquired what was in it. Quite innocently John replied rabbit. A look of horror came over Joe's face and he started yelling for John to throw the rabbit over the side, saying didn't he realise that rabbits on fishing boats were bad luck and that they would probably drown now! Many fishermen, particularly from Scotland, had this belief, and just the mention of the word rabbit was enough to postpone a fishing trip.

By the late 1930s large vessels of 40-50 feet began working from Paremata. One was the *Southern Cross*, owned by Tommy Isbister, and later by Jimmy Imlach. Another regular visitor to the port was the Island Bay boat *River Nile*, owned by the Tait family, and Jack and Artie Hunter also fished from there.

During World War II New Zealand Army personnel and US Marines were based at Paremata. Their presence affected the fishing operations for the local fishing community because of regular gunnery practice. A daily notice informing fishermen of any proposed gunnery exercises for that day was placed on a notice-board outside the store owned by Alf Iggulmdon, who also acted as honorary harbour master. Fishermen were required to check the notice-board and get a permit before sailing for their fishing grounds. For example, they may have been required to sail by 9.00 am and not return to port until 4.00 pm and certain areas were closed off as they were used as a firing range.

During early 1942 there had been a big run of snapper off the coast of Paremata. John Henderson and Alan Isbister of Cook Strait Fisheries had got a permit to go out for a day's fishing on the *Kate* and had departed their moorings by the specified time. As they were crossing the bar ahead of them they could see the *Wee Elsie* with Joe Foster aboard, also outward bound for a day's fishing. Suddenly one of the guns situated on the top of Mt Cooper (on the southern side of the entrance to Porirua harbour) erupted into action. With salvoes landing near the *Wee Elsie*, Joe was naturally startled and began waving his arms and jumping about with rage. *Wee Elsie* was hurriedly put about and returned to Paremata where Joe vigorously complained that the guns had been fired half

The early fishermen of Paremata's Hobson Street remembered

Above: Fishermen prepare to set their drag net in Pauatahanui Inlet, Porirua Harbour. (Henderson family collection)
Below: The fishing vessel *Pet*, owned by Thomson Bruce during the 1920s. The *Pet* had an unusual ram bow. (Henderson family collection)

Above: Paremata fishermen examine the contents of their drag net. Pictured from left: Dave Dement, Peter Isbister, Basil de Bakker, Jim Henderson and Alan Isbister. The girl is unknown. (Henderson family collection)

Below: The *Thistle* was typical of the early fishing vessels working from Paremata. It is seen here near Titahi Bay during a family picnic. Pictured on board are Gordon Henderson and his aunt, Doris Henderson, mother of John and Murray. (Henderson family collection)

an hour early. He was given an apology.

Occasionally unexpected visitors would arrive at Paremata due to bad weather. These were fishing boats from Island Bay, mainly owned by Italians. Because of the war these boats were under strict orders as to where they could fish and when they were to return to port. When the boats arrived in Paremata pandemonium broke out ashore as the authorities had to arrange for an armed transport to take the fishermen back to Island Bay until the weather conditions allowed the boats to return to their home port. Life was not easy for these fishermen, many of whom were New Zealand born. During the war some 38 Italians were incarcerated on Somes Island in Wellington harbour, remaining there up to five years. Wartime phobias were rampant during these difficult years.

As time went by the facilities improved at Hobson Street. By the early 1940s there were 21 baches in the 'street', the road was improved and trucks were able to drive down to pick up fish. There was now a grocery store in the street, owned by Tom Ryan, and life was a little easier for the residents. Families with children always had to be aware of their children's whereabouts as life for the young could be very dangerous with a railway track on one side of the street and the sea on the other.

In 1940 Alf and Sylvia Saunders settled with their children in Hobson Street, having purchased their home from fisherman, Julio Nervi. Alf was a master boatbuilder with a love of fishing. While living at Hobson Street Alf built a number of boats for fishermen, two examples being a 22-foot launch for Tommy Isbister and a 24-foot launch for a Mr Knight for fishing around Kapiti Island. Eventually Alf Saunders established a boatyard in the Hobson Street area and built many vessels for use in the fishing industry.

At the end of the war Paremata grew rapidly. By the mid 1950s major roadworks had begun in the suburb, for the old road had caused problems over the years and it was decided to straighten the road. By the late 1950s reclamation work was underway to straighten the railway line which originally ran behind Hobson Street. The reclamation began directly in front of the fishing community and it was inevitable that Hobson Street would also be reclaimed. This finally happened in the early 1970s. The realignment of the main trunk line and State Highway One took precedence over the little community of fisherfolk, boatbuilders and weekend bach owners, its character and history were gone forever.

This brief description of an early fishing community portrays one of many settlements that were established around the coast of New Zealand. The early fishermen of Paremata and others small communities were truly the pioneer fishermen of New Zealand's fishing industry.

References

Barbara Heath & Helen Balham, *The Paremata Story*,
Kapi-Mana News
Porirua Museum Oral History Collection
Wellington Maritime Museum Oral History Collection

Acknowledgements

John and Murray Henderson
Alf Saunders

Chapter Four
Alan Aberdein – Blue cod & crayfishing in the Chathams

I first met Captain Alan Aberdein in June 1994 aboard the MAF Fisheries vessel *Kaharoa* at its Queen's Wharf, Wellington berth. I had heard of his involvement in the fishing industry, particularly at the time of the crayfish bonanza at the Chatham Islands during the 1960s, and I was visiting the *Kaharoa* to see if Alan would allow me to record an oral history with him to be placed in the museum's collection of fishing history. After a very pleasant hour discussing many aspects of the fishing industry I left the *Kaharoa* with the promise of a future session. Sadly, a few weeks later, Alan told me that he had been diagnosed as having terminal cancer, although he was still very keen to speak to me. What follows has been put together from extracts of the oral history recordings made during Alan's illness and is an account of his life and involvement in New Zealand's fishing industry as he remembered it.

Alan Aberdein was born on 31 August 1934 at Aberdeen, Scotland. Deciding on a career at sea, he joined the British India Steam Navigation Company, which was then part of the P & O combine, as an apprentice deck officer. His first ship was the *Chantala* which he joined in March 1951 as one of 39 apprentices working and studying aboard.

The directors of the Picton Fishing Company. Left to right, Berry Chant, Alan Aberdein and Sandy Davies. (A. Aberdein Collection/ Wellington Maritime Museum)

The *Picton* at the Chatham Islands during February 1966. (B. Chant Collection/Wellington Maritime Museum)

Eventually, in 1955, he came out to New Zealand aboard the Union Steam Ship Company vessel *Kaponga* as third mate. His first ship on the New Zealand coast was another Union company ship, the *Kaiapoi*, in which he served for three months.

On leaving the Union company in 1956, Alan got his first taste of fishing. As he was walking along the viaduct at Auckland he met the skipper of the *Silver Sprays*, who asked if Alan fancied a holiday trip on his fishing vessel. Alan had never done any fishing before but, perhaps because fishing was an old tradition in Scotland, he seemed to take to it quite naturally. That holiday trip lasted six months!

After leaving the *Silver Sprays* Alan joined the *Coromel*, a converted cargo vessel, as second mate. This trip was a joint venture between Albert Meo, Pat Smith and Jim Jurie. The *Coromel* set off from Auckland in February 1956 bound for the Chatham Islands to act as a mother ship to some of the Chatham Island inshore blue cod fleet. The trip to the Chathams took 80 hours with the *Coromel* rocking and rolling all the way, leaving most of its crew seasick. It was not considered a good sea boat!

The first day's fishing was at the northern end of the Chathams; on that day the local launches transferred 14 tons of blue cod to the *Coromel* which was cleaned and processed on board.

After six months on the *Coromel* Alan joined the *Miro* as mate. Originally a sailing vessel, *Miro* was built by Bailey and Low at Auckland in 1925 for the Nobel Explosives Company to carry ammunition and explosives. Alan did two trips to the Chathams blue codding, then he returned to the big ships, mainly working for the Northern Steam Ship Company, serving as second mate and first mate on *Poranui*, *Tawanui*, *Tainui* and *Maunganui*.

Above: The *Tuhoe* as it appeared when owned by the Northern Steam Ship Company. The appearance was unchanged during its time fishing at the Mernoo Bank. (Wellington Maritime Museum Collection)

Below: Some of the *Tuhoe* crew haul in a longline by hand. (B. Chant Collection/Wellington Maritime Museum)

On leaving the Northern Steam Ship Company, Alan was asked by Andy Anderson, then working for the same company, to find a suitable ship for a coastal cargo service between Wellington and Kaiapoi, north of Christchurch, as Andy Anderson was proposing to set up a small shipping company. Eventually the coastal vessels *Toa* and *Tuhoe* were chosen and, with Alan Aberdein as a shareholder, the Kaiapoi Shipping Company was established in 1961.

The year 1962 was a significant one for coastal shipping in New Zealand as the roll-on roll-off rail ferry *Aramoana* was introduced, which decimated coastal shipping. Many small companies could not compete with this new concept of cargo handling. One of the many companies to suffer was the Kaiapoi Shipping Company. Some two years after it was formed, it was wound up.

What now? In 1963 Alan, Berry Chant and Sandy Davies, also members of the *Toa* crew, decided to go fishing. Arrangements were made to charter the *Tuhoe*, at £240 per week, and start fishing the Mernoo Bank which lies about 90 miles east-north-east from Banks Peninsula in the South Island. Before heading for the Bank to assess its productivity as a fishing ground, a small refrigerated railway wagon was put in the hold to chill any fish caught. Later, the hold of the *Tuhoe* was converted to a freezer. Cork was bought from a butcher shop in Wellington and taken to Kaiapoi where the conversion work was carried out. When completed the hold had a 15 ton capacity, not ideal but functional. Once the work was finished, it was time to catch fish! However, the weather had other plans. Three times the *Tuhoe* had to put back due to bad weather. Alan and the crew were getting a little anxious, as the charter period was for only one month and most of that month had gone without one fish being landed. Finally, with only days to go, *Tuhoe* was able to sail for the Mernoo.

The fish were biting from daylight, so quickly that the crew were hard pressed to keep up with the handlining. The crew worked two lines each with five hooks on each line. It was not unusual to have a cod on every hook each weighing 6-10 pounds. All the lines were then pulled up by hand! This was virgin ground and the fish were large and plentiful. Groper were also caught in large numbers, some up to 80 pounds. However, by the end of the day, another southerly gale developed and they decided to head for Wellington.

In one day the crew had landed nearly two tons of fish. This was sold to the Wellington Trawling Company owned by Albert and Lib Meo. They were impressed by the catch and happy to back the venture in the future. Although the first trip to the Mernoo Bank had encountered a few setbacks due to weather, Alan and the others were confident the venture would work. They formed the Mernoo Fishing Company with Alan, Berry Chant and Sandy Davies as directors. The crew of the *Tuhoe* were paid on a share basis and the directors paid themselves a nominal wage to allow the venture to establish itself.

Tuhoe continued to fish at the Mernoo for the next six months with fishing improving all the time. Other vessels followed the *Tuhoe* in fishing the Mernoo Bank: the *Venture*, owned by Jimmy Imlach, the *Neptune*, owned by Alan Isbister, the *Marlyn* and *Toa*.

After the initial six month period the *Tuhoe* had received a considerable battering so in 1964 they started looking for another vessel. At that time a vessel called the *Picton*, belonging to the Holm Shipping Company, was laid up. The directors approached

Berry Chant poses with one of the crayfish caught on the first expedition. (B. Chant Collection/Wellington Maritime Museum)

Captain John Holm offering to purchase the vessel. An agreement was made, with Captain Holm having £200 worth of shares in a £1000 company. The company was called the Picton Fishing Company Ltd. John Holm was very enthusiastic about this new venture and was to prove a very useful contact when the *Picton* started fishing in the Chatham Islands.

The *Picton* was built for the Richardson Shipping Co Ltd of Napier in 1917. Originally named *Koau*, it was built by Brown & Sons Ltd of Te Kopuru with dimensions of 87.7 feet long, 22 feet wide and 9.5 feet deep. When built *Koau* was powered by two standard OE Co. petrol engines, each developing 85 bhp. In 1952 it was sold to the Southern Cross Shipping Company of Picton (though managed by the Holm Shipping Company) who renamed it *Picton*. It was re-engined in 1955 with two 6-cylinder Gardner diesels each developing 114 bhp. The *Picton* was fitted with linehaulers and a freezer was fitted in the hold. The main hold had a 16 ton capacity, plus a wing freezer with a capacity of four tons.

The *Picton* and its crew of eight continued to fish on the Mernoo, though fishing there was very much subject to the weather. If bad weather developed, the *Picton* would be moved into deep water as sea conditions on the Bank became dangerous. It was because of this uncertainty that the *Picton* started fishing around the Chatham Islands. Alan preferred working there as they could work in most weathers in a vessel the size of the *Picton*. At different times of the year the Mernoo Bank and the waters around the Chatham Islands were infested with jellyfish

The *Moehau* setting crayfish pots to assess the crayfish potential at the Chatham Islands. (B. Chant Collection/Wellington Maritime Museum)

on which the blue cod fed. This made fishing difficult as the cod were too well fed and reluctant to take a baited hook. He also had a policy of only fishing for blue cod in areas not fished by the smaller local inshore cod boats, as he felt that having a large vessel he could find fish in less accessible places out of reach of the smaller boats. While fishing at the Chathams a number of locals were picked up to process the fish.

Fishing trips would last up to one month, depending on how long it took to fill the hold. The work was hard and the hours long and it was partly because of these hardships that the *Picton* was, in general, a happy ship. The crew that stayed chose to make the most of the situation and made a good living in return. One of the crew for a number of years was Steve Hrstich, known as Gypsy, who was the leading hand, a man Alan considered to be a very good and hard working fisherman. According to Alan, Gypsy's dream was to break the T.A.B. While the rest of the crew slept in cabins in the superstructure of the ship, Gypsy slept before the mast, preferring the fo'c'sle!

Line fishing was very productive with blue cod up to 13 pounds being caught, especially around isolated ridges. Occasionally great white sharks were caught, one shark brought in was 24 feet long. One of the grounds fished by the *Picton* was the 21 mile ground, also known as Inky's ground, after Johnny Inkster who had a processing factory at Kaingaroa. Johnny had told Alan Aberdein about it as the abundance of blue cod was making it difficult for him to catch crayfish. The blue cod were getting into his craypots and eating the bait. The ground was very productive and the *Picton* caught large amounts of blue cod, groper and trumpeter.

In the Chathams there were two methods

A good haul of crayfish comes aboard the *Norseman*, one of the many crayfish boats that were at the Chathams during the boom. (J. Inkster Collection/Wellington Maritime Museum)

One day's catch of crayfish, 6 tons, aboard the *Kingfisher*. The photo was taken in 1968. This type of catch was normal at the peak of the crayfish boom. (B. Chant Collection/ Wellington Maritime Museum)

of catching blue cod: hand-lining and cod pots. Using cod pots meant fewer crew were required with many tons of cod being caught in a relatively short time. On the *Picton* both methods were used, though hand-lining was preferred in the main. The *Picton* used six pots, usually with paua guts as bait. The pots were worked in rotation and would often come up with 500-600 pounds of fish. After emptying the pots into bins, the fish were headed and gutted before being packed in cartons ready for export, most of which went to Australia. Once full the *Picton* would return to Wellington, sometimes taking some of the cod caught by Chatham Islanders to sell.

After a few days in port, the *Picton* would head back to either the Chathams or the Mernoo Bank. On one occasion Alan was waiting for his crew to come back from the pub, before leaving for the Chathams. After waiting some time he went over the road to round them up. After some messing about the crew agreed to go, at which point the skipper had had enough and refused to sail. The next time in Wellington, Pincher Martin (whose brother Alfie had worked aboard the *Picton*) and Les Barber, executive officers of the New Zealand Seamen's Union, both thought it hilarious seeing the *Picton*'s crew carrying their skipper back to the ship so they could sail. Pincher thought it was the crew that held ships up, not skippers!

During his time at the Chatham Islands, Alan experienced relatively few accidents, with the most common being crew getting

Some of the *Picton*'s crew working their lines, including Len Weller (top), and Hughie Findlayson (middle). (B. Chant Collection/Wellington Maritime Museum)

One of five dories Alan was to own at the Chathams. (H. Goer Collection/Wellington Maritime Museum)

fish hooks stuck in fingers. Alan told of Joe Dicks, a crew member on the *Picton*, who got a fish hook in his finger and in an attempt to extract it, Alan put the shank of the hook into the vice and started cutting it with a hacksaw. After a short time the hook started to get very hot as did Joe's finger. At that point Joe had had enough and, grabbing his gutting knife, he cut the hook out and carried on fishing! They were a tough breed, those fishermen at the Chathams!

In 1965 Alan started taking building material and equipment down to Port Hutt for the Wellington Trawling Company. This was for the construction of a processing plant. Landing this cargo from the *Picton* was done with considerable difficulty as there were no wharf facilities. Fishing boats, surfboats and a barge were used to land the equipment, luckily without any serious accidents.

A fishing trip which had a major impact on the Chatham Islands occurred in June 1965. Alan had noticed that the crew, although fishing for blue cod, were foul hooking crayfish, some quite large. To see such numbers was, at the least, unusual. They decided this deserved further investigation and the ship's boat was sent off looking for crayfish. The men made good catches off Lion Rock, Pitt Island, and the *Picton* returned to Wellington with two tons of crayfish aboard.

On the next trip to the Chatham Islands Alan brought with him 15 crayfish pots. He approached Ron Brown, a local fisherman, who was operating the *Moehau*, then owned by the Picton Fishing Company, and asked him to work the pots. Alan offered Ron one shilling and sixpence per pound, which was accepted. After only a few days working the pots from the *Moehau* things were not going as expected and Ron Brown decided he and his crew would be better off working for a set amount. Alan agreed to this but on the condition Ron set the pots where Alan instructed. The next time Alan saw Ron Brown it was at the entrance to the Flower Pot, there was Ron working his pots in rotation and he had 500 pounds of crayfish aboard. Realising the earning potential, Ron asked if they could go back to the original agreement which they did. According to

Alan that's how it all started!

Naturally, landing the catch at Wellington caused a great deal of interest. As word spread of the bonanza, fishermen and boats, including the *Miro*, came from all around New Zealand and processing plants were built to cope with the huge influx of crayfish. At the height of the boom there were nine plants. Initially crayfish were tailed and processed to be exported mainly to the United States, with the bodies discarded at sea. Later, some of the plants processed the meat from the body and legs of the large male crayfish. Fishermen were not permitted to tail crayfish at sea, which caused considerable tension between the fishing community and the authorities, and Alan was involved in many a heated discussion regarding this matter.

As some of the processing plants had poor or non-existent berthing facilities, they found a novel method of discharging the crayfish from the fishing vessels. Helicopters, operated by Alexander Helicopters Ltd of Wanganui, were used at a cost of £1 per minute. Though expensive, the time saved in landing their catch was well worth it and allowed the fishermen to get back to their pots sooner. The helicopter went out to the boats with a large wire-mesh bin which could hold up to 1000 pounds of crayfish. The bin was suspended by 60 feet of rope and lowered to the deck of the fishing boat. Once the bin was full it was flown to the processing plant and landed on specially built platforms to be discharged. These bins could be jettisoned by the pilot in an emergency.

Most vessels worked 40-50 steel crayfish pots. These were set overnight on the edge of the foul ground and on the sandy bottom. Pots were set on the sand to catch the crayfish on the march and shifted to keep up with the moving crayfish. The pots would come up full of cray and sometimes not just full but with crayfish holding on to the outside of the pot. Bait for the pots consisted of fish heads, blue cod and paua guts. Other methods used to catch crayfish for a time were trawling and diving.

During 1966 22 trawlers trawled for crayfish in Hanson Bay which is on the eastern side of the Chathams. Working day and night, they landed 200 tons of processed crayfish tails in a matter of days. In 1968 the crayfish catch in the Chathams peaked; by 1970 it had substantially fallen.

There was a strong comradeship among those who fished at the Chatham Islands. Everyone helped each other as best they could. At the time of the boom there were boats fishing there from all over New Zealand. Some of these boats were not suited to the conditions at the Chathams. Not all skippers and crew had the experience to undertake such a venture and, as a result, a number lost their boats and their lives. Alan believed that there was an element of luck as some of the boats lost were very sound and had experienced crews. Many of the losses were during the voyage to or from the Chatham Islands. The more hazardous voyage was the trip back to New Zealand, as boats had been worked hard for some time and often required repairs.

Alan was involved in a number of search and rescue operations at the Chathams. One of these was the loss of the fishing boat *Karen* which belonged to Arthur Dickinson Jr. Unfortunately the vessel was lost with all hands. All the searchers found was the wreck on the southeast shore of Petre Bay. The *Karen* was a new vessel with all the latest equipment. It was the first of 20 vessels lost at the Chatham Islands during the four years of the 'boom'.

On another occasion the *Picton* received a

distress signal from a dismasted catamaran. Alan produced a coffee and cigarette stained chart and proceeded to lay a course towards the vessel using a cigarette packet. One of the crew stared at Alan in surprise to which Alan replied, "Sorry, mate, we're not in the Royal Navy". The outcome was a successful rescue, but little did the crew of the catamaran know of the role that Rothmans International had played in their rescue.

The Marine Department required boats to travel in convoy between New Zealand and the Chatham Islands. The early convoys were small but as the 'boom' got into full swing, the convoys got larger. Convoys assembled at Napier, Wellington, Nelson, Lyttelton and Timaru. Most convoys had relatively uneventful crossings, though some lost vessels and men. Alan Aberdein was in charge of a number of convoys, as the *Picton* was a large fishing boat and well suited to act as the lead vessel. The Marine Department required that each convoy have a lead navigator, second navigator and a qualified marine engineer. Convoys were ordered to steer clear of the Mernoo Bank due to dangerous conditions experienced there in certain weather. The voyage across would normally take about 52 hours, longer in bad weather. Vessels under 40 feet long were required to either be towed by a larger vessel or travel as deck cargo on the *Holmdale* which carried cargo to and from the Chatham Islands.

Above: The Picton Fishing Company letterhead.
Below: Alan Aberdein (in foreground of photo) hauls in blue cod aboard the *Picton*. (A. Aberdein Collection/ Wellington Maritime Museum)

It was while crayfishing at the Chathams that Alan was to experience a problem with one of the *Picton*'s propeller shafts which made it difficult to manoeuvre around some of the cray pots. The *Picton* was not the easiest vessel to handle at the best of times as one propeller was larger than the other, though according to other sources, Alan handled it easily. Alan purchased the 22 feet 6 inch fibreglass Marlborough Marine-built vessel *Patrick A* which was able to work the pots the *Picton* could not reach. *Patrick A* was paid for in five days!

The dory was the first of five bought by Alan; as well as the *Patrick A*, there were the *Albatross*, *Wendy Ann* and *Mariner*. Alan also had a 47 feet long steel vessel built, the *Rhona A*.

Parties were common during this time as hardworking crews had to unwind and Waitangi was the main watering hole. The *Picton* would spend the night in Waitangi at different times, and in Alan's opinion, some of the best parties were held at the policeman's house. Fights in the pub did happen, but not very often and usually between New Zealanders rather than the Chatham Islanders. If anyone was arrested for disorderly behaviour, they were locked up for the night until they sobered up and then returned to their boat. Sometimes they were required to do a bit of gardening before being released.

Alan and the *Picton* continued to fish at the Chatham Islands until the end of the crayfish boom in 1971. It ended almost as quickly as it had begun. Crayfishing was still viable but only for the local Chatham Island fishermen. Alan and his crew once again turned to blue cod fishing but the market was not as good as it had been, and he did not consider it viable to continue. He explored the possibility of crayfish being in sufficient numbers at the Campbell and Bounty Islands and he also went to the Auckland Islands for king crab. Unfortunately in all cases there was not enough fish to make it profitable.

January 1972 saw the end of Alan's involvement with the *Picton* and it was sold. (Eventually it was wrecked at Raoul Island on 20 July 1978 while under charter to the Ministry of Transport.) From then on he operated a number of trawlers out of Wellington, including the *Venture*, *Cerego* and *Moray Rose*. Alan had not had a great deal to do with this type of fishing, but soon proved himself fully capable and was having a fair success.

In 1978, after a spell ashore, he applied for a position as second mate aboard the MAF Fisheries vessel *James Cook*. This was to be another major turning point in his career. Alan had always had an interest in hydrography and marine life, as do most fishermen, and much of his underwater knowledge was gained by talking with divers who had worked at the Chathams. He found his new vocation interesting and challenging and felt he had successfully made the transition from catching to the research side of an industry he had been part of for so long.

Alan eventually joined the *Kaharoa* as mate and was later promoted to master of the vessel. Because of Alan's long involvement in the fishing industry, his knowledge in the field would have been invaluable to many of the scientists carried aboard.

Though I only knew Alan Aberdein for a short time, I found him to be the sort of person you feel comfortable with and who leaves you with a lasting impression. Many other people who knew him have told me of the high regard and respect they had for him.

Alan passed away peacefully at the Mary Potter Hospice on 22 October 1994. With his passing went a great deal of knowledge and the industry lost a good friend.

Acknowledgements

The Aberdein family
Duncan
Berry Chant
Harry Goer
Joe Gilroy

Chapter Five
Trawlers at war

During World War II many vessels of varying size and tonnage were chartered or bought by the New Zealand government and converted into minesweepers, danlayers and supply vessels. They were commissioned into the Royal Navy (the Royal New Zealand Navy from 1941). Some of the larger trawlers, for example the *Futurist, South Seas, Thomas Currell, James Cosgrove* and *Humphrey* served in World War I as minesweepers on both sides of the hostilities. In Britain and Europe the fishing industry has a long history of helping the nation in its hour of need.

At the onset of World War II New Zealand's fishing industry was quickly assessed by naval authorities. In September 1939 the Shipping Requisitioning Emergency Regulations came into force which provided for the hire of vessels at an agreed rate. If the company that owned the vessel disagreed with the terms, the matter could be settled by arbitration. Regulations were amended on 29 November 1939 to enable the government to acquire vessels by compulsory purchase.

The Marine Department requisitioned three vessels owned by the fishing company

A vessel which proved unsuitable for naval service was the *Phyllis*. Before being requisitioned for war service it had been involved in the whaling and fishing industries. On being declared a war surplus it returned to fishing. (Tudor Collins photograph: copyright V.H. Young & L.A. Sawyer)

A gunnery exercise aboard HMNZS *Waiho* which was a New Zealand built World War II 'Castle' class minesweeper. At the end of the war it was sold to Red Funnel Trawler Pty Ltd, Sydney, Australia. (Tudor Collins photograph: copyright V.H. Young & L.A. Sawyer)

Sanford Ltd of Auckland. The *Humphrey* and the *James Cosgrove* were stripped of fishing gear and delivered to the navy at Devonport in Auckland where they were converted into minesweepers. The other Sanford company vessel requisitioned was the *Thomas Currell*. However, it was on the fishing grounds at the time and, not having a radio, was unable to be contacted to report to Devonport until it returned to Auckland.

The *James Cosgrove* was a World War I Castle class minesweeper while the *Thomas Currell* and the *Humphrey* were Strath class minesweepers, which served in Britain during World War I. The latter two were originally built for the Royal Navy and were sold at the end of the war to be converted into trawlers. All three were brought out to New Zealand to become part of the Sanford company's fleet in 1920, 1922 and 1928 respectively. At the time the company was the premier fishing company in Auckland and one of New Zealand's major fishing companies, as indeed it still is.

Conversion of the vessels took five weeks. Though initially on charter all three were purchased in December 1939. The purchase price for the vessels, including fishing gear and spare parts, was £22,500.

The James Cosgrove was manned by naval personnel while the *Thomas Currell* and *Humphrey* had a mixed crew of merchant seamen (members of their original crew) and naval personnel. The skippers of *Thomas Currell* and *Humphrey* were given a temporary naval rank and remained in

The end result after a mine had been swept was normally an explosion caused by rifle fire. No doubt there would have been quite a large number of fish floating about belly-up after such an explosion. (Copyright T.W. Collins)

command of their vessels. The *Thomas Currell* was under the command of Lieutenant J. Holt, RNR, and the *Humphrey* was commanded by Lieutenant A.G. Nilsson, RNR.

Two other vessels requisitioned in the early stages of the war were the *Futurist* and the *South Seas*. The former was owned by New Zealand Fisheries Ltd and fished out of Wellington. At that time it was catching 30% of Wellington's fish supply. *Futurist* was originally the German minesweeper *Papenburg* which served during World War I.

The *South Seas* was owned by the South Sea Fishing Company Ltd and fished out of Lyttelton on the Chatham Islands grounds. Originally called the *Ferriby* it was built in 1913 for James H. Collinson of Hull by Goole Shipbuilding and Repairing Company Ltd of Goole, England. It was a Royal Navy minesweeper during the years 1915-19.

Both vessels were required to continue fishing so they only received partial conversions which enabled them to continue about their business. As a result of the sinking of the passenger liner *Niagara* on 19 June 1940 after striking mines 15 miles east of Bream Head, they were commissioned into the navy and conversion completed. Even though both vessels were on the fishing grounds at the time, they reported for full conversion within days of being "called up".

All five vessels were armed with 4 inch guns which were mounted on the foc's'le. Other weapons carried were two machine guns (Lewis or Bren guns) and depth charges.

While operating as boom gate vessels (vessels that opened and closed a gate which allowed access to harbours), the *James Cosgrove, South Seas* and *Futurist* were fitted with ASDIC systems which could detect the presence of submarines.

The purchase of the three Sanford trawlers by the government was to cause the company some major problems in supplying its customers with the fish they required. In 1940 the company was having great difficulty meeting the government contract for supplying fish to the armed forces.

In an attempt to rectify matters the company endeavoured to acquire trawlers both within New Zealand and overseas, but without success. This example of difficulties experienced by a fishing company was felt throughout the industry during the war years.

Some fishing companies with government contracts had the advantage of being able to commandeer fish landed from other markets or smaller fishing companies. Naturally, this would make them most unpopular, but it was necessary to help the war effort.

Manning levels during wartime varied depending on whether the vessel was minesweeping or danlaying. If serving as a minesweeper, a crew of 21-24 would be carried. If danlaying, the crew would be reduced to 14-18. These vessels would normally carry a crew of 10. The extra crew carried during wartime was accommodated in what was previously the fish hold.

The launching of HMNZS *Waikato* at the yard of Mason Bros Engineering Co. Ltd Auckland on 16 October 1943, one of the 13 minesweepers built for the navy in New Zealand. In 1944, when almost complete, it was declared a war surplus and passed on for disposal. It was better known as the fishing vessel *Taiaroa* (Tudor Collins photograph: copyright V. H. Young & L.A. Sawyer)

The sinking of the Canadian Australasian Line vessel *Niagara* was the catalyst for more fishing vessels being requisitioned or purchased by the government. The *Niagara* sank with 590 gold bars aboard, most of which has been recovered. Fortunately all 339 passengers and crew were rescued. *Niagara* is seen here at Auckland before the outbreak of World War II. (Wellington Maritime Museum)

Fishermen who wanted to stay with their vessels had to join the navy and undergo naval training. Fishermen were well suited to the life of minesweeping as, in principle, it was similar to trawling.

Other trawlers which were requisitioned or purchased during the early stages of the war were the *Nora Niven* (NZ Fisheries Ltd Wellington), *Phyllis* (Canterbury Steam Trawling Company Ltd) and *Coastguard* (Australian Fish Meal Oil & Hide Company Ltd).

The *Coastguard* was not as large as the other vessels mentioned so it was converted into a danlayer – a supporting minesweeper laying danbuoys after an area had been swept of mines, thus marking a clear channel for shipping. Though owned and registered in Australia and built originally for shark fishing in Australian waters, the *Coastguard* had been fishing out of Auckland since 1936. It was requisitioned without protest from the Australian government.

Prior to the sinking of the *Niagara* the three Sanford company vessels purchased by the government, along with the naval vessel *Wakakura*, were the only minesweepers in service. Though mainly deployed on patrol in the Hauraki Gulf carrying out routine minesweeping, they were also sent south to sweep other ports. Minesweeping consists of towing a wire astern of the vessel with an otterboard or paravane attached. As the trawler steams ahead the wire cuts through

Above: A pioneer in New Zealand's fishing industry and veteran of World War I, the *Nora Niven* was not suitable for naval duties during World War II due to its age. It only served for a short period then returned to fishing. (Tudor Collins photograph: copyright V.H. Young & L.A. Sawyer)

Below: HMNZS *Waipu* built by Stevenson & Cook Engineering Co Ltd, Boiler Point, Port Chalmers and launched on 31 July 1943 is typical of the Castle class of World War II. After the war it became part of the Sanford Ltd fleet. (Tudor Collins photograph: copyright V.H. Young & L.A. Sawyer)

Above: HMNZS *Coastguard* as a danlayer. It remained in the Royal New Zealand Navy fleet until 1960. (Wellington Maritime Museum Collection)

Left: One of the first trawlers requisitioned for the navy was HMNZS *Humphrey*, seen here on patrol.
(Wellington Maritime Museum Collection)

the wire that attaches the mines to the seabed. The mines then floated to the surface where they were exploded by rifle fire. After the sinking of *Niagara* the First Minesweeping Group was formed. In November 1940 vessels were allocated to Lyttelton and Auckland and were sent to other ports as required. Within a year permanent allocations followed.

Life on board these vessels was very routine, though they did have the odd mishap, such as breakdowns, collisions and lost rudders. The most serious of these was the sinking of the *South Seas* after colliding with the inter-island ferry *Wahine* in Wellington harbour on the 19 December 1942. Fortunately there was no loss of life.

As the war progressed other merchant navy vessels were requisitioned by the government. In 1940 the Marine Department decided to have some purpose-built minesweepers constructed. These would be based on the World War I Castle class minesweeper of which the Sanford company vessel *James Cosgrove* was one example. The vessels were built in New Zealand, some were of a composite nature (steel frames and wooden planking), others were built of steel. At the conclusion of the war many of the 13 warbuilt minesweepers were converted to trawlers both in New Zealand and abroad. Names such as *Maimai, Hautapu, Waipu* and *Taiaroa* (originally HMNZS *Waikato)* were well-known among the fishing industry well into the 1960s.

The trawlers *James Cosgrove, Humphrey, Thomas Currell, Nora Niven, Phyllis* and *Futurist* all returned to the fishing industry at different times during the war. Some proved to be unsuitable due to age or layout. Though a great deal of hardship was experienced by the temporary loss of these vessels to their owners, there is no doubt that those old trawlers helped to fill a very important role at a time which was difficult for most of the world.

Lieutenant Axel Nilsson, RNR. Born in Sweden in 1879, he was a wellknown skipper in the Sanford company fleet and considered an expert seaman and very competent trawler man. He served with the navy until his sudden death in January 1942 at the age of 63. (Photo courtesy of Sanford Ltd)

References

R.J. McDougall, *New Zealand Naval Vessels*, 1989

Paul Titchener, *The Story of Sanford Ltd: The first one hundred years*, 1981

S.D. Waters, *The Royal New Zealand Navy* 1956

Chapter Six
Maimai – from warship to trawler

The steam trawler *Maimai* began life in Port Chalmers in the yard of Stevenson and Cook Ltd in 1943. A vessel of 272 tons, it was 125 feet long by 23 feet wide and 14 feet deep.

Named after a river at Reefton on the West Coast, *Maimai* was commissioned by the Navy on 15 September 1943 as a World War II Castle Class minesweeper, and arrived at Wellington on 11 October 1943. It joined the 95th Minesweeping Group. Its duties during the war consisted of gunnery, depth charge and anti-submarine exercises and patrols. It carried out regular sweepings of the port entrance and exercised with and escorted submarines and other visiting warships. Though life was fairly routine, an anxious time was had in March 1944 when *Maimai* accidentally fired a depth charge thrower while berthed at Picton. Fortunately the depth charge did not explode. It was later recovered by navy divers.

In 1945 *Maimai* was disarmed but remained in the Navy for ammunition dumping and de-storing the outlying stations around Cook Strait and the Marlborough Sounds. It was finally de-stored and handed over to the Marine Department for disposal on 18 June 1946. *Maimai* was then sold to John Anderson of Wellington in the name of the Maimai Trawling Company Ltd. It began

HMNZS *Maimai* seen in 1945 during an exercise in the Marlbourgh Sounds. (Wellington Maritime Museum)

fishing in September 1946.

So began the career of one of the largest trawlers in New Zealand at the time. Its skipper was John (Jock) Cardno, a sturdy Scotsman from Inveralochy, Aberdeenshire. He went to sea on his uncle's herring boat at the age of 13. He lived and breathed fishing and sat his mate's ticket at the age of 19. Four years later he gained his skipper's ticket. Jock Cardno arrived in New Zealand during the 1930s and joined the trawlers *Futurist* and *Phyllis* working as a deckhand. He became a skipper in 1940. A very religious person, he was quoted as saying, "In Scotland no fishing is done on Sunday. We intend to observe that custom here too."

The engineer on the *Maimai* was Jack Sellers. It carried a crew of 10 in total.

Heaving the codend alongside, prior to it being split and the catch then lifted aboard. Pictured from top to bottom are: Jock Cardno, Gordon Dixon, Roy Coulston (Davis) and Jack Collins. (National Archives, Head Office, Wellington)

Fishing trips would usually start in the early hours of Monday and last until Friday. Fishing mostly took place between Wellington and Napier, Cape Turnagain and Castlepoint, Kaikoura and Cape Campbell and, of course, Cook Strait. The main fish targeted was tarakihi though groper, red cod, shark, crayfish etc. were often caught. Shark livers were also kept and sold to Karitane Hospital for use as a baby food supplement. For many years Jock Cardno held the record for landing the largest catch in New Zealand and between the years 1947–49 he recorded some of his best catches; his best was 1000 cases of tarakihi caught in 36 hours with ten hauls on the grounds south of Cape Campbell. The crew on that particular trip were J. Cardno, J. Sellars, B. Pullen, A.M. McDonald, W. Winters, J. Slater, R. Merrick and H. Finlayson.

During some of its early trips *Maimai* caught catches of 360 and 400 cases of fish in 14 hours. One case would hold 100–120 lbs.

During those early years Jock Cardno was greatly assisted by his wife who was a skilled net maker. At a time when it was very difficult to obtain codends, she made them by hand. This was common practice back in the 'old country' as women were heavily involved in the fishing industry. Three of Jock's sons followed their father into the industry, all three having worked at different times on the *Maimai*.

The *Maimai* was a side trawler; shooting the gear would take approximately 30 minutes, and would be towed for three hours. The net was 120 feet long. When the trawl was heaved to the surface, the bag or codend would be hauled alongside where the bag would be split and lifted aboard, then emptied into the pond where it would be sorted into size and species. After that the catch would be gutted, as all fish at that time

Maimai — from warship to trawler

Above: The *Maimai* as a trawler on the fishing grounds. (T.G. McBride, Wellington Maritime Museum Collection)
Below: John Summers was one of many engineers to work on the *Maimai*. He is seen here standing by the main engine controls. (National Archives Head Office, Wellington, AAQT 6401 A69 741)

Above: Crew at work repairing nets on board the *Maimai*. (Wellington Maritime Museum Collection)
Below: Back row, left to right: ?, John Cardno, ?, George Gardiner, ?, ?(the engineer); front row, left to right: Hughie Finlayson (fireman), ? (the cook), ?. (Wellington Maritime Museum Collection)

Above: What it's all about — the codend with its healthy load is swung aboard. (National Archives, AAQT 6401 969 763)
Below: The skipper (right) and some of the crew 'gutting' prior to the catch being sorted, boxed and stowed down below. (National Archives)

had to be, then boxed and stowed – a very labour intensive job. As this routine was continued around the clock, men were often on deck for 48 hours at a stretch.

The cook would work from 6 am to 6 pm and earn £10 a week clear. The boy was paid £5 per week. In 1947 fishermen were paid 4 pence a pound for top fish and 1½ pence per pound for rough fish.

During its early fishing years the *Maimai* was coal fired. In an average trip it would burn 35 tons of coal at £3 a ton. On one occasion the *Maimai* had to sail to Westport to load coal as there was a strike on at Wellington and the coal was bought at £1/2/6, which no doubt pleased the skipper who was one of the company's major shareholders.

During its career as a fishing vessel the *Maimai* became popular with those who worked on the Wellington waterfront. Its berth was close to the heart of the city at Queens Wharf outside the head office of the Wellington Harbour Board, now the Wellington Maritime Museum. Passers-by would often gather to watch the crew discharging the fish onto the truck which carried the fish to the Townsend and Paul Ltd's premises in Allen Street, Courtenay Place for processing and sale.

On most trips a few cases of fish were set aside under the heading of charity and these were given away to different organisations.

As the years rolled by catches started to get smaller and the vessel needed to catch over two hundred cases of fish to break even. Conditions on board were also deteriorating. With smaller and more efficient vessels being built at the time (which is rather ironical considering that the attitude is now bigger rather than smaller) it became harder to get a crew. Rather than not sail, the vessel would go shorthanded with the missing crew member's work load being shared among the crew as well as his share of the catch.

Finally at the end of 1966 the *Maimai* was sold for breaking-up and was scrapped in Wellington at the patent slip by Pacific Scrap Ltd. Age and modern technology had caught up with it, for although it was built in 1943 the design dated back to World War I. Many fishermen started their fishing careers in the *Maimai* and vessels of its class; all will have mixed memories of the ship and their ship mates.

Many 'landlubbers' also still remember these vessels and in many respects they are better known than their modern counterparts. Long may they be remembered.

Acknowledgements

John Cardno, Jnr

References

R.J. McDougall, *New Zealand Naval Vessels*, 1989

The *Maimai* being broken up for scrap on the patent slip in Evans Bay. (Wellington Maritime Museum Collecton)

Chapter Seven
The life of the *Thomas Currell*

When built in 1919 the *Enrico,* as it was then known, was a state of the art steam trawler. Built by R. Williamson & Son in England it was one of many 'Strath' class trawlers built during and after World War I. A vessel of 115.2 feet in length, with a beam of 22.1 feet and a draft of 12.2 feet, it had a gross tonnage of 203.77 tons and was powered by a coal fired 430 hp steam engine. It could carry a crew of ten.

In 1921 Sanford Ltd of Auckland were expanding their fleet of fishing vessels. They heard of several trawlers available in England and sent representatives to look over the vessels. The *Enrico* seemed to fit the company's needs and was purchased. The new owners changed the name to *Thomas Currell.* Some alterations were made and spare equipment, such as an extra propeller and shaft, were loaded and the vessel left England for the long voyage to New Zealand.

It was a difficult voyage, with rough weather experienced for much of the way. The *Thomas Currell* arrived at its new home port of Auckland in February 1922 after three months. Although the voyage had been long and hard the master described the *Thomas Currell* as an excellent sea boat. It was put to work and soon proved itself.

By 1930 Sanford Ltd had four steam

Below: The *Thomas Currell* leaves its berth at Auckland in 1946 for the fishing grounds. (Photo courtesy of Sanford Ltd)

The *Thomas Currell* shortly after being re-engined heading out into Wellington Harbour for engine trials. (*Dominion* Collection)

trawlers in its fleet: the *James Cosgrove, Thomas Currell, Humphrey* and *Serfib*. It was at this time that the government imposed restrictions regarding vessels trawling within the Hauraki Gulf. Trawlers were prohibited from working inside a line between Cape Rodney and Cape Colville from 16 November through to 16 March. This restriction was brought about because it was felt the large trawlers were damaging the fish stocks. Sanford trawlers now had to steam much further to fishing grounds in the Bay of Plenty and East Cape areas. This combined with the onset of the Great Depression to reduce profits from the trawling operation. The Depression meant a serious downturn in trade. To remain competitive, prices were cut and by 1932 two of the trawlers were laid up because of oversupply.

During this time the *Thomas Currell* continued to fish for the company. At the outbreak of World War II, the trawler was at sea and unaware of the declaration of war as it was not fitted with a radio. In those early days most trawlers did not carry radios. Some, including the *Thomas Currell*, had a novel means of communication: the carrier pigeon! Vessels were fitted with aviaries behind the wheelhouse and when fishing was over and the vessel on its way home a pigeon would be released. A message would be attached to its leg informing the owners how much fish had been caught.

On returning to Auckland a week after the declaration of war, the *Thomas Currell* discharged its catch and shifted to the Devonport Naval Base as it had been commandeered by the government along with the *James Cosgrove* and *Humphrey*. The three vessels were converted for minesweeping duties. Each was fitted with a 4 inch gun, depth charges and minesweeping gear, as well as a wireless telephone and telegraph equipment. The work was carried out by the naval dockyard at Devonport. The first of the Sanford trawlers to be commissioned for service was the *James Cosgrove* on 10 October 1939. The *Humphrey* and *Thomas Currell* followed six days later. These three vessels were the first in New Zealand to be commandeered at the outbreak of World War II for service as minesweepers.

Initially the *Thomas Currell* and the two

other Sanford vessels were on charter to the government. The charter system proved very costly and made business difficult for Sanford Ltd. In November 1939 the regulations were amended to enable the government to purchase the *Thomas Currell, James Cosgrove* and *Humphrey* at a cost of £22,500.

During the war HMS *Thomas Currell* had a fairly routine service, mainly searching and sweeping for mines which had been laid by German raiders operating around the coast of New Zealand. Most of HMS *Thomas Currell's* naval service was spent in Auckland sweeping the Hauraki Gulf and during this time the vessel found a number of mines laid by the Germans. At other times the *Thomas Currell* was sent to other ports to sweep for mines.

One incident involved the RMS *Niagara*. On the morning of 19 June 1940 a distress signal was received from the passenger liner *Niagara* reporting it had struck a mine between Bream Head and Moko Hinau Island and was sinking. The *Thomas Currell* and the *James Cosgrove* were ordered to sea and proceeded at full speed. They arrived in the vicinity of the sunken *Niagara* at 12.50 pm. Their minesweeping gear was deployed and at 2.48 pm the *Thomas Currell* reported a mine in its sweep. Shortly after the *James Cosgrove* also reported a mine. Both mines were freshly painted and had not been in the water very long. They were contact mines which explode on contact with a ship's hull. Both were destroyed by rifle fire.

In September 1944 HMNZS *Thomas Currell* was paid off from the newly formed Royal New Zealand Navy and in January 1945 the vessel was sold back to Sanford Ltd and refitted for trawling. Difficulties were experienced during the refit as there was a scarcity of materials required to complete the work and it was not until late 1945 that the vessel was again ready for fishing.

By the early 1950s Sanford Ltd were entering a new phase of their development. No longer were the large steam trawlers seen as an economic method of fishing. The price of coal had escalated and crews were becoming harder to find as the vessels were

A certificate of shares in Combined Fisheries Ltd belonging to Jim Winton. (Wellington Maritime Museum Collection)

The *Thomas Currell* on the fishing grounds in Cook Strait. (Wellington Maritime Museum)

now rather dated. The trend was towards smaller vessels with smaller crews and lower running costs, so Sanford's decided to put the *Thomas Currell* and two other steam trawlers up for sale.

It was at this time that the manager of the Wellington Fishermen's Co-operative, Salvi Dellabarca, approached Tom Brown and Chris Sotiri, respectively president and vice-president of the Wellington Fish Retailers Association, and Johnny Di Mattina with a proposal to purchase a large trawler to ensure a regular supply of fish for the Co-op, retailers and customers alike.

The Wellington Fishermen's Co-operative was set up during the depression of the 1930s by fishermen of the Eastbourne and Island Bay communities as a means of selling their catch at a more profitable price. In its day the Co-op was one of the major fish wholesalers in the country (see Chapter Two).

After the *Thomas Currell* was examined by Salvi Dellabarca, John Campbell and Jim Winton, the vessel was found to need some hull repairs, and after some negotiations an agreement was reached whereby the work was carried out in the Devonport dry dock by Mason Engineering Ltd. When this was finished the *Thomas Currell* left Auckland under the command of John Campbell, with Jim Winton as engineer, for its new home port of Wellington.

A subsidiary company of the Wellington Fishermen's Co-operative was formed and given the name Combined Fisheries Ltd. Combined Fisheries was a company made up of a number of equal shareholders: the Wellington Fishermen's Co-op, fish retailers consisting of 25 shops, the skipper, John Campbell, and chief engineer, Jim Winton.

The skipper, John Campbell, was an experienced fisherman and well known in Wellington. Born in 1911 on the Island of Lewis on the west coast of Scotland, he went

The life of the Thomas Currell

HMS *Thomas Currell* on patrol in the Hauraki Gulf during World War II. (Tudor Collins photo: copyright V.H. Young & L.A. Sawyer)

to sea at the age of 15 aboard a herring boat. The work was hard with many miles of net being set each night and later being hauled in by hand. At the age of 22 he left the fishing industry, and travelled to London where he joined the Royal Mail Line. Eventually he joined the New Zealand Shipping Company vessel *Rangitane* on which he came out to New Zealand where, at the age of 27, he decided to settle.

After a brief spell ashore he once again went fishing, joining the steam trawler *Nora Niven* and later the *Futurist*, both fishing out of Wellington. With the outbreak of World War II both vessels were commandeered by the government and their crews paid off. He then worked at the Patent Slip in Wellington, eventually shipping out again on Union Steam Ship Company and Holm Shipping Company cargo vessels. At the conclusion of the war he once again returned to fishing, joining the steam trawler *Hautapu* as skipper.

Though he liked shipping out on cargo vessels he was at his happiest when he was fishing. It was in 1952 that he was approached by Salvi Dellabarca about the skipper's position aboard the *Thomas Currell*, a position he soon accepted.

At the time the company purchased the *Thomas Currell* licences for large vessels of this type were difficult to get. The Fishermen's Co-op had to assure the Marine Department that the venture would ensure the supply of fish to the local market at a reasonable price before they would grant a licence. According to Lib Dellabarca, who was responsible for distribution at the Co-op, Wellington fish retailers were among the best supplied in the country, mainly due to the joint involvement of the Fishermen's Co-op and Combined Fisheries Ltd.

The main target of the *Thomas Currell* was tarakihi which was caught in the Cook Strait, Kaikoura, Akaroa and Wairarapa fishing grounds, depending on the time of year and the weather conditions. During the winter fishing continued around the clock providing the weather was suitable. In the summer fishing was done during the day with the vessel hove to during the night. Some 30% of the fish caught was supplied to the Wellington Fishermen's Co-op. The rest was distributed among the retailers. Retailers who were shareholders in Combined Fisheries were guaranteed a quota of the catch.

In common with all the steam trawlers working out of Wellington at the time, the fishing trip would start at 12 am Monday morning and normally last until the early hours of Friday with the catch being discharged that morning. Steam trawlers berthed at Queen's Wharf and Friday mornings were a busy time with the trucks belonging to wholesalers and retailers hurrying about with their cases of fish.

Upon discharging their catch the trawlers were washed down and the gear mended ready for the next trip two days later.

Many years of service had taken their toll

Skipper John Campbell on the bridge of the *Thomas Currell*. (John Campbell Collection)

on the boiler and it was becoming very expensive to operate. In 1955 Salvi Dellabarca decided to have the *Thomas Currell* re-engined. The conversion was carried out at Wellington under the supervision of the then chief engineer, Fred Abernethy. At the time the conversion was believed to be the first on a vessel of that type in New Zealand or Australia.

The steam engine and boiler were removed and a 480 bhp Blackstone Lister diesel engine was fitted. Due to a 20 ton difference in weight, ballast had to be put aboard to give the ship better stability. It was estimated that the new engine would give the vessel 25 days duration at sea. The cost of the refit was £20,000.

With the refit the outward appearance of the vessel also changed: gone was the tall funnel behind the wheelhouse. Instead a smaller squat funnel was placed further aft. This made the *Thomas Currell* look slightly odd as it no longer had a balanced profile. Nevertheless, looks were unimportant against the vessel's ability to catch fish.

In the late 1950s there was a change in management of the Wellington Fishermen's Co-op. This had a detrimental effect on Combined Fisheries, so much so that it eventually led to the company's demise and the *Thomas Currell* was offered for sale. One of the shareholders in Combined Fisheries, Jim Winton, purchased the vessel. He continued to work the trawler from Wellington and renamed the company T.C. Fisheries Ltd, selling the catch to the Wellington Trawling Company Ltd. Approximately two years later he leased the *Thomas Currell* to the Wellington Trawling Company with the option to purchase after a two month period. The *Thomas Currell* was sold for the sum of £10,000.

In 1966 at the time of the crayfish boom at

Above: The Blackstone Lister being gently lowered into the *Thomas Currell's* engine room. Fred Abernethy was chief engineer and responsible for the installation. (Fred Abernethy Collection)

the Chatham Islands, the *Thomas Currell* was sent to Port Hutt, Chatham Islands, to act as a freezer depot. Crayfish was stored aboard and later brought over to mainland New Zealand by the *Holmdale*. While the *Thomas Currell* was moored at Port Hutt, it was maintained by Jimmy Lenaghan. He had been the chief engineer on the voyage to Port Hutt and was appointed manager to the processing plant which belonged to the Wellington Trawling Company at Port Hutt.

Jimmy was born in Scotland and served in the Royal Navy during World War II. Here in New Zealand he had worked as an engineer/fisherman on numerous trawlers and was well known on the coast.

At different times the *Thomas Currell* broke free of its moorings causing Jimmy Lenaghan considerable anxiety. Finally, in 1968, Jimmy decided he would rid himself of the problem and ran the *Thomas Currell* ashore at full speed at Port Hutt. Jimmy Lenaghan was keen to claim to be the *Thomas Currell's* last skipper/engineer.

The *Thomas Currell* still lies where Jimmy beached it, a reminder of times gone by. Many years have passed since the purchase by Sanford Ltd but its varied role during those early years means the *Thomas Currell* is truly representative of New Zealand's fishing history and won't be easily forgotten.

References

P. Titchener, *The Story of Sanford Ltd: the first one hundred years,* 1981

R.J. McDougall, *New Zealand Naval Vessels,* 1989

S.D. Waters, *The Royal New Zealand Navy: New Zealand in the Second World War,* 1956

Acknowledgements

F. Abernethy, J. Campbell, L. Dellabarca, J. Lenaghan, J. Winton.

The *Thomas Currell* as it appeared after engine conversion, seen here coming up Wellington Harbour on return from the fishing grounds. (National Archives ref. AAQT 6401 A69746)

The remains of the *Thomas Currell* ashore at Port Hutt, where Jimmy Lenaghan left it after purposely running it ashore in 1968. (Jim Winton Collection)

Chapter Eight

The early years of commercial fishing in Taranaki

Jim Rutherford, now aged 90 years, has had a lifelong interest in fishing. Born on 1 March 1905 at Wanganui, he grew up at Waverley in Taranaki. His father ran a flaxmill in the town. Jim went to Waverley Primary School until the age of twelve when he was sent to live with his grandfather at Pihama where he completed his primary school education. Growing up in Pihama started his interest in fishing as there are several rivers in the area and his uncle kept a small boat at the Oeo river mouth. On completing Standard Six he was sent to Nelson College where the name Rutherford was well known and respected. Both Jim's father and uncle attended the college. Jim's uncle, Ernest Rutherford, was the noted scientist who first split the atom.

On leaving Nelson College he was offered a position in a bank, but was persuaded to work on the family farm at Pungarehu, as it was presumed the farm would be his one day. While living there Jim would go fishing off the

Jim Rutherford aboard the *Annabella* at its berth at Port Taranaki, New Plymouth. Ngamotu Beach is in the background. (J. Rutherford Collection/Wellington Maritime Museum)

Port Taranaki and New Plymouth during the late 1940s. The breakwater affords some protection to shipping, though in very bad conditions large vessels have to leave the port. (Wellington Maritime Museum Collection)

coast with one of his friends, Kira Ramati, who was skipper of a 30 foot whaleboat. Whenever Kira had difficulty in getting a crew he would call on Jim or his brother Alan to go out with him. Kira, his crew and Jim would go fishing along the coast catching snapper, conger eels, blue cod, small sharks and the occasional groper, sometimes fishing all night.

Jim remembers that before going out fishing the Maoris would light small fires at each end of the boat which they believed would bring them good luck. Like some of the European fishermen who settled in New Zealand, there were certain words which they considered bad luck and which were not spoken before or during fishing. They also usually returned the first fish to the sea or secured the fin from the first fish to the whaler's bow.

Much of the area fished was rocky with reefs running out off the coast. They used handlines with metal hooks, though some traditional gear was used at times. One unusual piece of equipment consisted of a small tree branch which had four or five branches of its own. On each branch was attached a snooze and a hook. This equipment was used for catching fish over rocky ground.

Returning to the beach near the Pa could at times be dangerous as the coast was very

Left to right: Jim Rutherford, Bernie Frewin and Eric Bain aboard the *Elsie* off Gannet Island. Eric Bain was aboard visiting from the fishing vessel *Campbell*.
(J. Rutherford Collection/Wellington Maritime Museum)

exposed and there was a heavy surf. The boat was swamped occasionally, though not when Jim was aboard and fortunately without loss of life. On arrival the boat was met by a number of Maoris who were keen to see what had been caught and who helped to haul the boat back up the beach. The fish was distributed among the inhabitants of the Pa, then Jim was offered a fish to take home.

The Depression

During the early 1920s farming was at a low and, with the high prices paid during World War I gone, many farmers walked off the land. Among them was Jim's family and Jim took up flax cutting and farm work in the Manawatu. At the start of the Great Depression the flaxmill closed and Jim returned to New Plymouth. Eventually he got a job stacking butter at the cool stores, earning £3/14/- for a 44 hour week.

As this was a seasonal job, Jim found himself out of work for 3-4 months of the year. Occasionally he was able to get work for a day or two loading meat onto ships for export to Britain. It was during this time that he got the opportunity to buy a 20 foot launch fitted with a benzine engine. When the weather was favourable on the weekend, Jim would go out fishing four or five miles along the coast from New Plymouth. He would arrive at his fishing ground in the mid-afternoon and would handline for snapper, fishing until the early hours of the morning. Arriving back in New Plymouth on Sunday afternoon, he would sell his catch to people at Ngamotu Beach where his launch was moored. Snapper were all sold for a shilling each, regardless of size, with the average weight being approximately seven pounds. He soon found he was earning more money from one night's fishing than he made stacking butter for one week.

The *Elsie*

It was during those difficult days of the Depression that a friend of Jim's, Bernie Frewin, an unemployed builder and a World War I veteran, approached Jim regarding a partnership in a fishing vessel. Bernie had been offered work pushing a barrow for £1 per week but this was not enough to sustain him and his family. Jim agreed to the partnership and they began looking for a larger vessel. They heard of a vessel for sale at Whangarei called the *Elsie*, 38 feet in length and with a cockpit. They bought it for £250 and took it to New Plymouth, stopping along the way to catch a load of snapper. On arrival it was slipped. Bernie flush decked it as the cockpit limited their movement, and

The *Geneva May* arrives at Port Taranaki for the first time. Its voyage across the Tasman Sea had been uneventful. Standing in the doorway is Alan Rutherford. The two men on deck were picked up in Sydney for the delivery.
(J. Rutherford Collection/Wellington Maritime Museum)

installed a fish hold.

Jim and Bernie fished between New Plymouth and Kawhia and every 5-6 months they would take the *Elsie* into Kawhia for painting and antifouling. The *Elsie* was run onto the beach at high tide, painted and hauled off on the next tide.

Before heading off to the fishing ground they caught fish for bait, mainly kahawai and barracouta, off the Sugar Loaves near the port of Taranaki. Fishing trips were normally overnight, if the weather allowed they would go out for two days. The best time to catch snapper was the evening and into the night until the early hours of the morning.

Each man worked two hand-lines while the vessel drifted. In shallow water a stray-line was used which consisted of two hooks and a line without a sinker. Hand-lines with sinkers were also used. This gear was made up with a large sinker, normally a railway line fishplate and 5-6 hooks. As the vessel drifted, it was followed by schools of snapper eating scraps of bait which had fallen overboard. On one occasion they got so close he was able to gaff a number of fish. This was during the months from October to February when spawning snapper were found close to the surface.

During the early 1930s there were only a few commercial fishermen working from New Plymouth and they were lucky enough to secure a regular customer for their catch. Each week they had to supply 1000 pounds of fish to a Mr McAsey who, each Friday, would supply fish to the Catholics at Opunake. They also sold to three fish shops in New

Plymouth. At times they had trouble selling their snapper to other shops in the area as their fish tended to be slightly larger. Most of the shops were supplied with snapper caught in the Auckland area which were trawled and a smaller size. On Sundays, Jim and Bernie sold their fish on the wharf as many people would be strolling along the waterfront, though this did not impress some of the fishmongers. The fish, gilled and gutted, were never sold for more than one shilling each. However, Jim and Bernie felt it was too good an opportunity to ignore. Both were earning £15 per week which was outstanding during the Depression of the 1930s.

Working for the Harbour Board

In 1936 Jim married; his wife was not very keen on him going to sea and, with the effects of the Depression easing, Jim was able to get a job with the Taranaki Harbour Board. It was his job to shovel shingle from the beach and mix concrete for the building of large concrete blocks for the breakwater extension. Bernie had also gone ashore, back to the carpentry trade. They kept the *Elsie*, using it on weekends to catch a few fish to supplement their incomes. Jim had bought himself a Harley Davidson motorcycle and sidecar which he used to carry ice to the boat, as well as fish. It could take around 500 pounds. During the Depression the wholesalers paid two pence a pound for gilled and gutted snapper, paying an extra halfpenny per pound in the winter. Hapuku and crayfish earned three pence a pound.

While working for the Harbour Board Jim was called upon to act as an able seaman or fireman on the Board's dredge *Paritutu* when the vessel travelled to Wellington to undergo survey. He enjoyed these trips, though conditions on board were rather spartan. On one particular trip they were caught in a southerly gale and could make little headway. The engineer informed the captain that their supply of coal was getting low and he doubted if they would have enough to get to Wellington. The captain ordered the engineer to burn the timber lining in the coal bunker. Some hours later the engineer appeared on the bridge once more and asked the captain which wing of the bridge he should start dismantling! Fortunately the weather eased and enabled the *Paritutu* to make for Picton where it loaded coal from the hulk *Edwin Fox* and continued to Wellington.

Building the business

With the onset of World War II Jim served as an officer in the New Zealand Army, training

Alan Rutherford mending the net aboard the *Geneva May*. (J. Rutherford Collection/Wellington Maritime Museum)

at Waiouru in tank warfare. Eventually he was to see action at Guadalcanal and be promoted to the rank of major in charge of his unit. When the war ended Jim returned to New Zealand and was discharged three weeks later. Having accumulated a few pounds during his service he was keen to return to fishing. He realised that the best prospect for a good future for him and his family lay in that industry. Jim heard of a vessel at Wellington which was for sale and went to inspect it. The *La Reine* was 40 feet long, powered by a Fairbanks-Morse diesel engine and built by Lanes of Picton. As part of the rehabilitation scheme for returned servicemen, it was inspected by the Marine Department free of charge and was found to be in excellent order. Jim bought it and, with his two crew, delivered it to New Plymouth.

Jim arranged to sell his catch to Jack Kurta, a fish wholesaler in New Plymouth, and commenced fishing operations. Once again Jim line-fished, mainly targeting snapper and groper. Without sophisticated fish finding equipment, he used three handlines set at different depths to establish at which depth the snapper were running. During his earlier years of fishing, Jim had kept a daily log in which he recorded the weather conditions where he was fishing and how much fish was caught. He found his log books a useful tool to guide him to the best fishing areas at particular times of year.

When a good haul of snapper was aboard Jim and his crew would gut and gill the fish and bundle them, using a brass needle and string, into bundles of six or seven fish. These were then stowed below on ice. The ice was bought in 56-pound blocks which was crushed and layered on the fish. Jim remembers that often they would return to port with 2½ tons of snapper which had been caught overnight!

A Move to Trawling

After two and a half years of working the *La Reine* the demand for fish had increased considerably and Jim felt that he needed a larger vessel. Eventually a suitable vessel was found in Timaru. The *Annabella* was 50 feet long, powered by a Gardiner diesel engine and built by Miller and Tunnage Ltd of Port Chalmers. Jim enlarged the fish hold and prepared it for fishing. The *La Reine* was kept until the new vessel was working properly and then sold.

Trawling was a new method of fishing for Jim. With his experience in line fishing, Jim knew where many of the reefs and other obstacles were situated and this meant he didn't foul his net very often. There were some problems: Jim was catching fish, but not the number of snapper he should have caught. In an attempt to solve the problem Jim went down to Lyttelton to seek advice from the well known fisherman George Brassel. Jim was taken out off Akaroa aboard George Brassel's *Tawera*, where they came to the conclusion that the design of the net was at fault. It was suggested to Jim that he contact a net maker in Auckland by the name of Munro who was well known for his skill. He eventually sent Jim a trawl with a larger square which would catch the snapper as they lifted and tried to get out of the way of the trawl. The new gear proved very successful and the problem was solved. Some of the other species of fish caught were tarakihi, John Dory, rig and gurnard, though the latter was not very popular during the late 1940s.

The equipment used on trawlers at the time was not as sophisticated nor as durable as it is today. The floats used on the trawl were initially made of glass and would often break due to the water pressure. The net itself was mainly cotton, to help preserve the

The *Calm* ashore at Waiweranui Point near Cape Egmont. The anchors laid by Jim Rutherford played a major role in salvaging the ship. (Wellington Maritime Museum Collection)

codend it was tarred and nets had to be dry before storing as they would rot if stored damp for any length of time. When trawling off Patea in the South Taranaki Bight, Jim would place a number of floats in the codend to help keep it off the bottom which was very rough in places.

It was while fishing with the *Annabella* that Jim was to experience his closest brush with disaster. They had been fishing off the coast of Waitara in bad weather and, having just lifted a large bag of fish, were struck by a large sea that knocked the *Annabella* on its side. At the time Jim and some of his crew were preparing the catch for stowing below in the hold. Jim managed to hold on until the *Annabella* righted itself. When it did, it had a 15 degree list and was swept clean of the fish on deck and any equipment not securely lashed down. There was flooding below and the engine was nearly awash but still operating. After a struggle Jim was able to start the pumps which soon dealt with most of the water. The list was caused by some of the vessel's ballast shifting when it had rolled on its side. They eventually made it back to Port Taranaki where the ballast was shifted back into place. Jim had every confidence in the *Annabella* and considered it an excellent seaboat.

In the early 1950s Jim's fishing career took another turn. Business was going very well, so he convinced his brother Alan to bring his family out from Britain and settle in New

Plymouth where they could become partners in Jim's fishing venture. Alan Rutherford had been an oil driller working in Britain and Iran for the Anglo-Iranian Oil Company and had helped to develop a number of oil fields. He accepted Jim's offer and, not long after, the brothers expanded into fish wholesaling in New Plymouth.

Salvage

In the early hours of 14 July 1956 Jim received a telephone call from the Port Taranaki Harbour Master, Captain John Flett. The coastal cargo vessel *Calm*, owned by the Canterbury Steam Ship Company, had run aground in gale force conditions at Waiweranui Point, six miles north of Cape Egmont lighthouse. The vessel had left Port Taranaki the day before and, heading into the teeth of a southeasterly gale, the master had decided to return to port but had run aground. Jim was requested to stand by in case the *Annabella* was required.

Annabella sailed at daybreak for the stricken *Calm*. The passage was rough but it handled well. On arrival Jim was informed that the crew were safe. A tug was sent for from Wellington and the *Annabella* was to take a barge with kedge anchors and cables to the *Calm* where it would lay the anchors in preparation for salvage. Meanwhile cargo from the *Calm* was discharged to lighten the vessel before the salvage attempt. With the arrival of the Union Steam Ship Company tug *Taioma*, Jim eased the *Annabella* and punt in towards the *Calm* and laid the anchors which were to play an important role in the salvage of the ship. It was later revealed that when the *Calm* had gone ashore, the light on Cape Egmont had gone out because of damage caused to the powerlines by the gale. The light was unmanned and no one realised what had happened.

Jim's local knowledge and boat handling skills were obviously well known to Captain

A good haul of snapper caught off Patea by the *Annabella*. (J. Rutherford Collection/Wellington Maritime Museum)

Flett who had himself been a fisherman and skipper of the fishing vessel *Manuka*. In situations such as this, fishermen and their local knowledge are often called upon to assist.

The year 1956 was also significant for the Rutherford brothers personally, as their business expanded further when they purchased the 55-foot fishing vessel *Geneva May*. Jim had inspected the vessel while on holiday with his wife Molly in Australia. In an uneventful voyage, Jim and Alan, plus two crewmen, sailed the vessel across the Tasman Sea from Sydney to New Plymouth. In later years the *Geneva May* was re-engined with one of two Gardiner diesel engines which had been originally purchased to re-engine the lake steamer *Earnslaw*, but it had been decided the *Earnslaw* would remain a steam vessel. Both vessels worked well and the supply of fish to their wholesale business increased dramatically.

Jim recalls the large numbers of foreign vessels fishing off the Taranaki coast in the late 1950s when New Zealand only had a three mile offshore territorial limit. Many boats were also seen fishing within the limit. He feels that during those days more should have been done to prevent this happening. Successive governments ignored the potential of the country's fishing resources. In areas where in the past he had caught 1000 pounds of fish per tow, he was now catching 200 pounds.

Life ashore

Eventually Jim came ashore and ran the wholesale side of the business, and two skippers were appointed to run the company's vessels. Alan had begun a project to build a steel vessel on Ngamotu Beach which was to be completed as the stern trawler *Margaret J*.

In 1962 Jim Rutherford was elected to the Taranaki Harbour Board. His knowledge of the port, having worked both ashore and afloat, was a definite advantage in his duties as a board member. As far as he is aware he was the first fisherman elected to the Board. Serving on the Works Committee, Jim was able to convince the Board and its executive officers that it was more cost-effective to extend the breakwater of the port using the board's own tradespeople, who had previously been involved in its construction. The extension was completed under the estimated contract price. Jim served as a member of the Board for 15 years during which time he believes he was able to make a useful and constructive contribution.

After many years in the fishing industry the Rutherford brothers decided to sell their business in 1972. Jim retired and Alan went on to use the *Margaret J* as a service vessel for the large iron sand vessels loading off the Taranaki coast.

Though Jim worked in other industries and learnt many skills, the time spent fishing were his happiest working years. However, he never forgot the knowledge gained elsewhere and these skills helped make him one of the practical people who were so important during the early pioneering years of fishing in New Zealand.

Acknowledgements

Jim Rutherford

References

Gavin McLean, *Canterbury Coasters*
A.B. Scanlan, *Harbour at the Sugar Loaves*

Chapter Nine
The middle years of commercial fishing in Taranaki

Loui Kuthy was born in Szegad, then the third largest city in Hungary, in 1924. Szegad is on the banks of the river Tisza and the young Loui soon developed a keen interest in the river and fishing. Loui's passion for fishing rather surprised his parents who could not understand his interest in such a messy pastime.

The river produced a variety of fish and there were sufficient numbers to sustain a small commercial fishery. This consisted of a number of small boats setting fish traps. Loui recalls that as a boy, he saw a catfish weighing 82 kilos landed by one of the fishing boats.

In 1956 the Hungarians revolted against the Soviet domination of their country. It was a period of huge unrest and 175,000 Hungarians, including Loui, fled the country. Leaving his job as managing director of a large government owned transport firm, Loui went to Austria where he hoped to immigrate to Australia as a refugee. Unfortunately the Australian quota had already been filled so he opted for New Zealand instead – a decision he has never regretted!

Loui arrived in Auckland in January 1957, unable to speak a word of English, and was sent to Eltham in Taranaki to work in the rural sector. After a short time he moved to New Plymouth where a number of Hungarians had settled. Almost immediately he obtained a job as a wheelbarrow man, then became an orderly at the hospital, and with time he began to learn to speak English. During this time Loui maintained his interest in fishing, by surfcasting off the beach and watching the fishing fleet and recreational craft coming and going from Port Taranaki.

Eventually he got to know some of the recreational fishermen and was invited to go out for a trip, an offer he enthusiastically accepted. Loui soon became a regular day

Loui Kuthy, not long after his arrival in New Zealand, during a fishing contest at New Plymouth. (L. Kuthy Collection/Wellington Maritime Museum)

Loui Kuthy, right, standing alongside the truck he used to carry his catch from Wanganui to New Plymouth during the early years of his operation, with his father who was visiting New Zealand from Hungary. (L. Kuthy Collection/Wellington Maritime Museum)

tripper. Having got the taste for sea fishing, Loui bought a small runabout which he used until it broached and capsized coming in through the surf at Paritutu Beach. Luckily for Loui and a Hungarian friend of his, they were good swimmers and were able to swim ashore. Later he bought another boat and continued his favourite pastime.

An opportunity

Watching the commercial boats heading out to the fishing grounds off the Taranaki coast made Loui's interest stronger and he began to look seriously at a career as a fisherman. He was given his chance by Jim Rutherford, a well-known New Plymouth fisherman. Though Loui had no commercial fishing experience, Jim agreed to take him on aboard his vessel, the *Annabella,* on a trial basis. Jim soon realised that Loui was highly motivated and extremely keen to learn all he could. Loui could earn up to £80 a month, which was very good money as the average pay ashore was approximately £10 per week.

Loui found the long hours gutting, gilling and bundling fish between hauls of the trawling gear quite different from his previous day trips. There was little sleep to be had during these trips which would last 3-4 days. Luckily Loui did not suffer from seasickness which meant he could concentrate on learning and doing his job.

After two years on the *Annabella* and *Geneva May,* Loui and a partner, Max Auntunovic (aided by Dr James Dempsey who made funds for the venture available through an unsecured loan), purchased a trawler from Auckland called the *Norman McLeod.*

The *Norman McLeod* was built in 1942 and originally used to service lighthouses for the Marine Department. The vessel was later put up for sale and purchased by two ex-servicemen who operated it from Paremata near Wellington as Paremata Fisheries Ltd. Later the *Norman McLeod* was sold to Doug Munro and Ken Turner who worked the vessel from Auckland for ten years. Loui and Max bought the *Norman McLeod* from

Jim Rutherford's pride and joy, the *Annabella*, was the first commercial fishing boat on which Loui worked. (L. Kuthy Collection/Wellington Maritime Museum)

Munro and Turner and found their new vessel was an excellent sea boat, with a hull made of three skins of kauri and teak. Loui continued to operate under the Paremata Fisheries Ltd name, and it was not until some years later that he changed the name to New Plymouth Fisheries Ltd. At the time he acquired the *Norman McLeod*, Loui was not a New Zealand citizen and because of this he was not permitted to operate the vessel's radio and had to relay messages through the crew.

Building a business

Loui mainly worked the *Norman McLeod* from Port Taranaki supplying whole fish to fish shops throughout the Taranaki region. During the early 1960s he concentrated on working the Patea/Wanganui fishing grounds where snapper and trevally were plentiful. Trawling operations were conducted at night and Loui recalls that the area was so productive that it was not unusual to fill the boat in one night!

As he was spending so much time fishing in the South Taranaki Bight, Loui decided he could save a lot of steaming time by basing the *Norman McLeod* at Wanganui and giving himself the maximum fishing time possible. The *Norman McLeod* would take approximately 10 hours to reach the fishing ground from New Plymouth. Loui based a truck in Wanganui, loaded his catch and drove to New Plymouth where he distributed the fish among his customers. Fishing from Wanganui was only a temporary measure as Loui's fishing licence and boat registration

The *Norman McLeod* working off the Taranaki coast with a big bag of snapper alongside. (L. Kuthy Collection/ Wellington Maritime Museum)

were issued for Port Taranaki and his customer base was there.

During those early years Loui occasionally found it difficult to sell his catch. The export market was in its infancy and local demand was not high, unlike today where fish is professionally marketed and has been scientifically proven to be healthy eating. Loui believes that during those early years catching the fish was the easy part and that your operation could only be as big as your market, which in those years was mainly fish and chip shops. He believes fishermen had to ensure they came home with the popular fish species or they would not sell their catch. Fish such as gurnard, trevally and rig were practically unsalable in large numbers. Gurnard and red cod were dumped over the side because of lack of demand, something he looks back on with regret.

During the summer when the snapper were running in large shoals he would catch large numbers, and invariably he would be left with excess fish after providing his 25-30 customers. In an attempt to sell the surplus he would visit motor camps in the region, towing a trailer behind his Ford 10, loaded with iced, gilled and gutted fish and shouting at the top of his voice, "Fresh snapper for sale." He would make good sales until lunch time by when the fish did not look so inviting due to the heat and the losing battle with flies.

In those days the only outlets in the area were fish and chip shops and if Loui could not persuade them to take a few extra bundles the fish had to be dumped. Loui can still visualise large, plump snapper being dumped over the side with lumps of ice still attached, slowly sinking to the depths. In his words, "it was a shameful waste".

As trawlermen know, net mending is a never-ending task. Loui Kuthy is in the foreground along with Frank Roper. (L. Kuthy Collection/Wellington Maritime Museum)

In 1969 Loui purchased another vessel. The *Alf Amor* was 32 feet long of the Windex design, powered by a 175 hp diesel engine. The vessel was purchased to fish for crayfish on the newly found ground in the North Taranaki Bight.

Unfortunately the vessel was to be wrecked on the night of 3 February 1970. The *Alf Amor* had been laying at anchor sheltering from bad weather along with the *Norman McLeod*, half a mile off Waikawau Beach near Awakino. Due to the rough conditions the two-man crew transferred to the *Norman McLeod*, skippered by Loui, until the weather eased. However, during the night the anchor cable parted and the vessel drifted ashore where she was wrecked.

Pair Trawling

In 1971 Loui took a trip back to Europe for a holiday. While in England he heard about pair trawling being conducted from one of the English fishing ports. He found this method of trawling interesting and believed it would suit certain areas around New Zealand. On returning to New Zealand in 1972 he was anxious to pursue the matter further and found out that experiments were being conducted in the Bay of Plenty and the Hauraki Gulf. He learned of two vessels, the *Seawyfe* and the *Brothers*, which were doing experimental pair trawling from Tauranga. He travelled to Tauranga and spent a few days with their skippers and crews discussing their experiences in pair trawling. They were happy to pass on details of their findings and Loui returned to New Plymouth determined to introduce this type of trawling to Taranaki.

At that time the fishing vessel *Geneva May* had just come on the market. Loui bought the *Geneva May* from David Urquhart who had bought the vessel from the Rutherford brothers, and set up his two vessels for pair trawling. Both vessels were ideally suited to this method of trawling, having identical engines: 8 cylinder Gardners with 3 to 1 reduction gear boxes. A new era of fishing was about to begin from Port Taranaki!

As well as the *Geneva May*, Loui also acquired a small processing plant at Waitara with a limited capacity chiller, also from David Urquhart. On 4 April 1972 Loui, with his two partners, W.C. Watts and S.N.

A bag of snapper about to be emptied aboard the *Norman McLeod*. Pictured are David O'Donnell on the left and skipper, Eric Parker. (L. Kuthy Collection/Wellington Maritime Museum)

Gillbanks, formed Fresha Fisheries Ltd. Loui owned 70% of the company and his partners had 15% each. They were able to get a loan to buy and upgrade the plant and retail outlets because of the projected catch increase when they changed to pair trawling.

After equipping the two vessels for pair trawling the new venture began in earnest. The *Geneva May* and *Norman McLeod* were operated by three crews on a rostered system to enable the vessels to be at sea for the maximum time and still allow the crew to get regular time off. Loui was one of the skippers, the other two were Watts and Eric Parker. Gillbanks acted in the capacity of sales manager and ran the marketing side.

Initially they experienced a few teething problems with gear and training the crews in the new fishing technique. When using the traditional trawling method the gear is towed directly behind the boat and the mouth of the net spread open with otterboards or trawldoors. With pair trawling the mouth of the net is much larger, as is the overall length of the net compared to the gear used on similarly sized trawlers engaged in a single vessel trawling operation. The mouth of the net is spread by both trawlers running parallel some distance apart, eliminating the use of trawldoors thus reducing drag through the water. Heavy weights are used to get the trawling gear down onto the sea bed. This part of the operation is crucial and was one of the major problem areas. In Loui's words, it "had to be experimented with to perfection".

Eventually they ironed out all the problems and landed some excellent catches at New Plymouth. The most notable of these early catches was landed on 30 August 1972 when the *Norman McLeod* and the *Geneva May* landed a record catch for Port Taranaki of 70,000 pounds of fish. The catch was made over two and a half nights fishing on the South Taranaki Bight and was only the third pair trawling trip.

The down side

All was going well until an unfortunate chain of events struck the company. Their first misfortune was the grounding of the *Norman McLeod* north of the Waiwakaiho River on

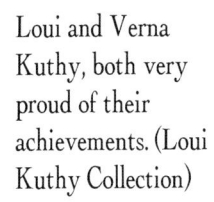

Loui and Verna Kuthy, both very proud of their achievements. (Loui Kuthy Collection)

the night of 9 February 1973. The *Geneva May* was able to tow the stricken vessel off at high tide. Though only slightly damaged the vessel's propeller blades were bent and after inspection it was decided to take the vessel to Nelson where repairs could be carried out.

Initially repairs were supposed to take about two weeks, but instead Loui was faced with the nightmare of having the *Norman McLeod* out of the water for two and a half years! A water-logged area in the hull was mistaken for rot and this meant the vessel could not get a clean bill of health until that section dried sufficiently for inspection by the Marine Department. Ultimately it was realised that in fact the vessel was sound; an apology was offered and the vessel allowed to return to fishing.

During the 2½ year period the *Norman McLeod* was laid up the company was forced to charter a replacement vessel to work with the *Geneva May*. This added to the costs incurred by having the *Norman McLeod* sideslipped and staff problems made the situation worse, placing further strain on the company's finances. Late in 1979 the company was put into receivership.

This was a devastating blow for Loui who had worked extremely hard to build up his company. "It was a very frustrating feeling knowing that despite all the potential we had, we would probably lose everything!" However, frustrated is not defeated and Loui convinced the Development Finance Corporation that his business was viable and sustainable, and they agreed to allow him to trade out of his difficulties. It was in those difficult days of early 1980 that Loui met his future wife Verna.

Verna

Verna had a good administrative background, with eight years in the Police Department and seven years in banking. When she volunteered to take over the management of the shoreside operation, the receivers welcomed her wholeheartedly. At this time she purchased Watts' share of the company, Gillbanks having sold out some time previously. By joining the company in an administrative role Verna enabled Loui to return to sea and together they made a concerted effort to work their way out of receivership. This took four years to achieve and Loui recalls it was one of the happiest days of his life when he rid himself of the stigma attached to receivership. In his words, "Today we look back with pride and satisfaction that we did not give in but with hard work and perseverance proved the authorities wrong!"

Fresha Fisheries Ltd once again began to grow, so much so that the processing factory in Waitara became too small. Loui and Verna started looking for larger and more suitable premises which they eventually found in New Plymouth. The new building had been used as a meat processing plant and was ideal for their operation, though extensive alterations were required to bring it up to the strict health standards expected for seafood processing and the export market.

On 8 November 1991 Fresha Fisheries Ltd opened their new head office and factory for business. Its situation is unusual as it is in the middle of a residential area, though the plant is discreetly out of sight and does not intrude on its neighbours. In a special opening ceremony, the Prime Minister, Mr Jim Bolger, officially opened the plant and stated that "this thriving business is living proof of a husband and wife bracing their shoulders in a common aim and achieving more than the imagination can."

For Loui and Verna it has been hard work but they feel what they have achieved has been well worth the effort and being the

Loui Kuthy with the Prime Minister, Jim Bolger, at the opening of the new plant on 8 November 1991. (Taranaki Newspapers Ltd)

largest fishing company in Taranaki means a great deal to them. They both believe the quota management system is one of the best things to have happened to the New Zealand fishing industry and believe the industry has an excellent future. The only aspect regarding the modern industry that Loui feels will hamper any young person entering the industry is the cost of buying quota to start up a business as he and others have been able to do in the past.

Still fishing

Today the company is still very much involved in pair trawling and Loui is still at the helm of the *Geneva May*. At 72 he could sit back and let skippers run both of his vessels, but he and Verna both prefer the "hands on" approach. They know working beside their employees keeps them in touch with any problems and helps to build a team, and it certainly helps to keep the "boss's" feet on the ground.

Nowadays there is a much greater public demand for fish. To fill this demand there are nine small vessels selling their catch to Fresha Fisheries, as well as the *Norman McLeod* and the *Geneva May* pair trawling. The smaller vessels are mainly gill netting, long lining and lobster fishing. Most of the seafood is sold on the domestic market with the rest being exported.

Alhough he immigrated to New Zealand with no belongings whatsoever (even the clothes he wore and the £5 in his pocket were generously given by the International Red Cross) but with a passion for fishing, Loui was determined to make a success of his new life. After 38 years in the industry he is now contemplating retirement and is proud of the contribution he and Verna have made to the fishing industry.

Acknowledgements

Loui and Verna Kuthy

References

Taranaki Herald
New Zealand Shipwrecks

A scene on board. (Loui Kuthy Collection)

Chapter Ten
Captain Charles Daniel: Master mariner – Fisheries Inspector

Charles Bamford Daniel was born in London, England, on 6 July 1883. At the age of three he came to New Zealand with his parents and two siblings. They settled in the Auckland area where his father was employed as a blacksmith's striker. At the age of 13 Charles left school and may have worked as a labourer until, at the age of 16, he went to sea as a deck boy on the sailing vessel *Southern Cross* which traded around the islands of the south west Pacific. On 10 July 1899 he paid off in Auckland, having returned from the Solomon Islands with malaria. His next ship was the *Wenona* which was employed between New Zealand and Australia. In February 1900 he went deep sea aboard the British barque *Star of the East*, joining it in Auckland as an ordinary seaman.

The ship was bound for New York via Cape Horn, returning to New Zealand four months later for another cargo. Sailing from Auckland, the ship anchored in Rangitoto Channel to wait for a favourable wind. Charles, however, was having second thoughts about the trip. Whether he was overcome by homesickness or was just reluctant to spend several more months at sea is not known, but he decided he did not want to stay and leapt over the side, swam to Cheltenham beach and made his way to his

Captain Charles Daniel as a fisheries inspector. Rock oysters can be seen on the rock behind him. (B. Daniel Collection/ Wellington Maritime Museum)

Charles Daniel first went to sea as a deck boy aboard the *Southern Cross*, later renamed *Ysabel* as shown in the photograph. (B. Daniel Collection)

parents' house at Devonport, or the 'Shore', as it was known at the time. Eventually he left for Thames where he shipped out as an able seaman on the sailing vessel *Margarita*.

Sail and steam

In 1906, at the age of 22, Charles Daniel passed his Home Trade Master's Certificate. From this point on he served in a variety of vessels, both sail and steam, as by the early 1900s sailing vessels were rapidly being replaced with steam ships. Some of the steam ships he served in were the *Hawea*, *Stella*, *Wairoa*, *Lyttelton* and *Clematis*. He also commanded a number of sailing scows which included the *Seagull*, *Welcome*, *Tramp*, *Rambler* and the *Ranger*.

Captain Charles Daniel, centre, his crew and his dog Rags, aboard the sailing scow *Rambler*, loading sawn timber at Mercury Bay in mid 1911. (B. Daniel Collection/ Wellington Maritime Museum)

Oyster Cultivation at Manaia in January 1932. (B. Daniel Collection)

It was during his command of the *Tramp* that the vessel had to be beached during a storm. During a voyage on the west coast of the North Island, from Kaipara to Manukau Harbour, loaded with kauri logs, they experienced deteriorating weather conditions which turned to gale force south westerly winds. Sails were reefed and an attempt was made to claw off the coast, but the scow was being swept by the huge seas. Captain Daniel decided the only chance of survival for his ship and crew was to beach the vessel. The captain ordered his crew aloft and, tying himself to the wheel, he squared the ship before the wind and following sea and headed for the beach. At 1 pm on 26 June 1907 the *Tramp* surfed ashore ten miles south of the Kaipara entrance with its captain and crew landing safely. Eventually the cargo of logs was removed and the vessel was repaired and returned to service. The *Tramp* was owned by the Ford Shipping Line, Auckland, and was a vessel of 95 feet in length, built by George Niccol at Auckland in 1902.

In 1910 Charles married and had a family. Not wanting to be away from his family for a great length of time, he found employment with the Devonport Steam Ferry Company as a master and commanded most of their vessels. Later he worked as a signalman at Hokianga Harbour, where he lived with his family during World War I. At the end of the Great War, in 1918, Charles and his family left the Hokianga and returned to Auckland where he joined the Marine Department as shipping master under Captain Atwood.

With the Marine Department

Charles Daniel was responsible for the signing on and off of crew, and became so good at his work he acquired the name of Shanghai Daniel. For those unfamiliar with the term, the word shanghai was used to describe a way of obtaining crew against their will, by getting them drunk or drugging them so they could be taken aboard ship, where they wouldn't wake up until they were well out at sea. Though Charles Daniel did not resort to these means, he was certainly not the sort of person to be ignored. He was known to round up recently signed-on crew, who had not reported for duty, from hotels or brothels around Auckland, put them in a taxi and personally deliver them to their ships.

A well known and respected figure in the Auckland maritime industry, by the early 1920s Charles Daniel once again changed his occupation. This time he joined the Fisheries section of the Marine Department, becoming a fisheries inspector in the Auckland area, in particular the Hauraki Gulf. As part of his duties he ran a fisheries protection vessel named the *ANZAC*. Due to the Hauraki Gulf's enormous size he would often spend days away from home patrolling parts of the Gulf.

One of the tricks he used to catch poachers unaware was to paint each side of the *ANZAC* two different colours. He would approach any suspicious boat in a friendly manner and study the offender, then steam away. Once he was behind a headland or sufficiently clear he would turn around and head back to the offending vessel, showing the other side and hoping not to cause any alarm. Once alongside, he would deal with the offence.

Danish seining in the Hauraki Gulf

With his new responsibilities as a fisheries inspector, Charles decided he needed to find out first hand how fishing was conducted in the Gulf. His knowledge as a seafarer was immense but fishing was a different world and one he had to master if he was to act with any authority. To gain this knowledge he went on a number of fishing trips with commercial fishermen who mainly used line, set net or Danish seining fishing methods. One of the fishermen he went out with was Jock McKay who owned a converted keeler

Charles Daniel, left, and Jock McKay, aboard the fishing vessel *Viola*, during the early days of Danish seining in New Zealand. (B. Daniel Collection/Wellington Maritime Museum)

The Fisheries inspection vessel *ANZAC* which Captain Daniel used to carry out his duties in the Hauraki Gulf. (B. Daniel Collection)

called the *Viola* which was a very narrow vessel powered by a 10 hp benzine engine. Without a large holding capacity, it was mainly used as a day boat. Working alongside the fishermen, Charles soon learnt how different fishing methods worked.

At this time, in 1923, Danish seining was a new method of fishing in New Zealand. It was through the efforts of the Auckland fishermen who used this method that it became so popular. From Auckland it spread to other parts of the country such as Nelson, Lyttelton and Napier. At the time it was considered an excellent means of catching fish. It allowed smaller vessels to make good catches, mainly of snapper, which were often comparable to catches made by larger trawlers. A Danish sein boat had much lower overheads when compared to the trawlers of the day. Having a crew of only 2-3 and smaller engines made them profitable.

Because of the efficiency of this method of fishing restrictions were introduced. In particular, the areas where fishing operations could be conducted were limited. Areas such as harbours, sounds and small bays were not considered suitable by the Fisheries Branch of the Marine Department. It was Charles Daniel's responsibility to patrol such areas in the Hauraki Gulf and enforce the regulations. No doubt, he did from time to time find someone flaunting the law, though fishing companies based in Auckland actively discouraged their skippers from breaking the law. When a vessel was found in a restricted area fines were imposed; for instance, illegally trawling in a prohibited area incurred a fine of £1 plus costs, and illegally taking whitebait £3 plus costs. Compared to today, the fines imposed were minimal.

During those early years of Danish seining most fishing was done near Waiheke Island in the Hauraki Gulf. The procedure began by dropping an anchor with a buoy attached to it with one end of a rope. The vessel was then steamed in a semi-circle, paying out the rope as it went until the required amount of rope was set. Then the net was set with the rope attached to one wing. Another rope was attached to the opposite wing and the vessel

Sacks of rock oysters being discharged from a truck into an Auckland Harbour Board shed. Charles Daniel is on the right of the photograph. (B. Daniel Collection)

steamed back to the buoy and secured to the anchor. The ropes were then winched aboard which hauled the net towards the anchored vessel. When alongside, the codend was lifted aboard and emptied. Initially the mesh sizes in the codend were small which meant smaller fish were caught. To reduce this, regulations were altered, increasing the size of the mesh. As Danish seining was so efficient, a number of steam trawlers were converted to this method of fishing. However, due to the size of the gear they were using, fish stocks in certain areas within the Hauraki Gulf were seriously affected. Recreational fishermen complained bitterly to government, who changed the regulations to force these larger vessels into areas which made this method of fishing uneconomical, so they returned to trawling.

A scientific interest

Life for a fisheries officer must have been quite hectic, with fisheries regulations and methods of fishing changing so rapidly during those early years. By the late 1920s skippers of fishing vessels in the Auckland district were issued with daily log books in which they would enter the day's catch. In previous years there had not been a clear record of fish being caught around New Zealand and this was seen as a way towards achieving an accurate record of the species and quantity caught. Auckland was the first to trial the new system and from there it would be introduced to other ports. It was not

Charles Daniel at work on a rock oyster farm at Manaia in January 1932. (B. Daniel Collection)

considered absolutely accurate but it was the first step towards achieving their goal. Over the years, the recording methods have been considerably changed with the introduction of new technology.

As time went by, Charles Daniel developed a keen interest in marine biology. He bought a microscope and started taking samples from a variety of fish. In 1927 work had begun on a study of snapper feeding habits. This was done as part of investigations into the impact of Danish seining on snapper. In 1928 Charles Daniel continued this research by examining the stomachs of snapper caught by commercial fishing boats. During the period July 1928 to March 1929 he examined 1940 snapper stomachs. It was found that the diet of snapper varied at different times of the year. Charles also observed a great abundance of snapper spawn in the Hauraki Gulf during the summer schooling season. He obtained samples of eggs by towing a small net or by using a bucket to scoop up eggs from near the surface. Placing some of the eggs in jars of sea water, he was able to hatch larval fish.

This interest in the reproduction of snapper, dabs and flounders, and the recording of his observations was invaluable to Marine Department scientists. One scientist he worked with closely was Mr M.W. Young, one of the pioneer researchers in experimental oyster culture and observation of the oyster in its environment. Some of the observations and experiments conducted by Charles Daniel in this field were of significant assistance to Mr Young, including one experiment which found that a water temperature of 19.8° Celsius was the best for the artificial impregnation of the ova of rock-oysters.

The development of oyster farms in the Auckland area was a major priority for the Fisheries section of the Marine Department. Experiments with different types of oysters had taken place with both successes and failures. As part of the effort to identify the best areas in which to set up an oyster farm, in order to get a higher yield, fisheries inspectors in charge of launches were required to keep a daily log of water temperatures and meterological conditions. This information was used to ascertain when the water temperature was appropriate for the spawning of oysters.

When not involved with his experiments, Charles was observing fishing vessels operating out of Auckland and inspecting fish markets. Eventually he became head of the fisheries branch of the Marine Department in Auckland. In 1944 Charles Daniel died at the age of 60.

During his 48 years of working life he experienced a variety of challenges and

The crew of an early Danish seiner at Auckland haul their catch of snapper alongside. (B. Daniel Collection)

achievements, each with its own satisfactions, though the years spent in the fisheries branch were probably the most fulfilling. While not a trained marine biologist, his enthusiasm, commitment and inquisitiveness made up for lack of formal training. His pioneering observations regarding snapper and oysters may seem minor by today's scientific standards but, in those early years of fisheries research, the information he gathered helped to develop fisheries we now take for granted.

Postscript

One of Captain Charles Daniel's sons, Barney Daniel, was interviewed for this chapter. He also has a maritime background and is a well-known character on the Wellington waterfront. During his working life he has been a wharf builder, shipwright, shipowner, master and owner of the old scow *Success*, which was used for many years to remove rubbish from visiting ships to Wellington Harbour.

Acknowledgements

Thanks to Barney Daniel for letting me interview him for this chapter. My thanks also to Pat Skinner, nephew of Barney, who has been compiling the Daniel family history, for making some of his research available to me.

References

B. Daniel, *A Kiwi Journal*
P. Titchener, *The Story of Sanford Ltd, the first 100 years*
Annual Reports of the New Zealand Marine Department

Chapter Eleven

The *Mobil Chatham*

The *Mobil Chatham* is not a vessel most people would readily identify as being a part of New Zealand's fishing history. But it has, in fact, played a part in both the whaling and fishing industries. An ungainly vessel, it was launched in January 1960 as the *Hinunui*. It was built by Cuddon's Products Ltd of Blenheim for the Perano whaling station at Tory Channel in the Marlborough Sounds and took four months to complete.

The Perano station was the last shore-based whaling operation in New Zealand, though the region has a long history of whaling. The *Hinunui* was designed to transport whale oil from holding tanks at the whaling station to vessels anchored in Tory Channel. The tanker was built with three compartments and had pumping equipment built into it. At the time of its construction it was one of the largest projects of this type undertaken in Marlborough. As a whale oil tanker, its capacity was 65,000 gallons of oil. The vessel's dimensions were 72.1 feet long by 14.3 feet wide by 14.25 feet deep.

The *Hinunui*, not long after its launching into the Opawa River at Blenheim. The launch towing the tanker belonged to T. Eckford & Co. Ltd. (Courtesy *Marlborough Express*)

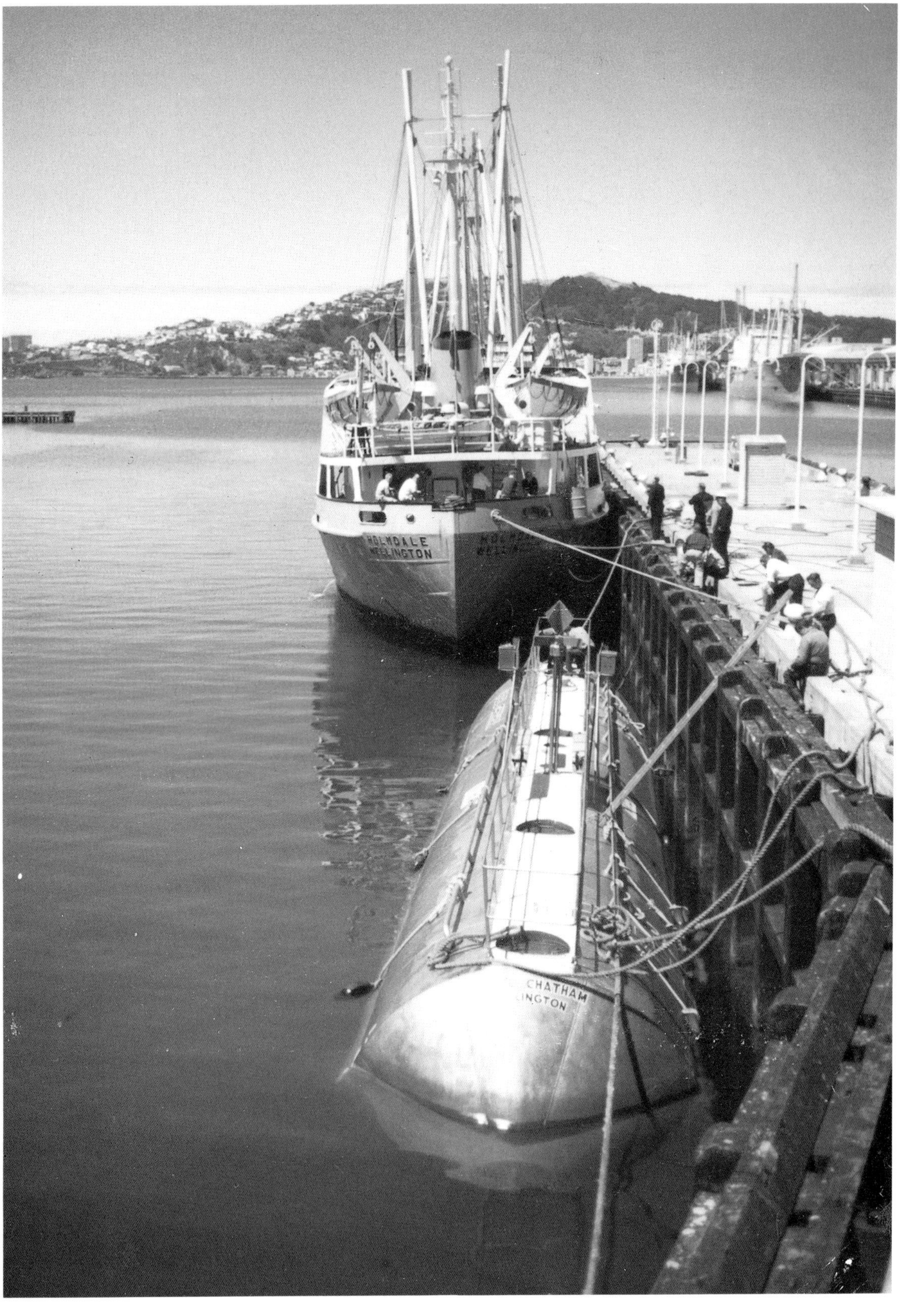
HOLMDALE
WELLINGTON
CHATHAM
LINGTON

The Mobil Chatham

Left: The *Holmdale* and *Mobil Chatham* at the rail ferry terminal, preparing for the voyage to the Chatham Islands. Above: The *Holmdale* and *Mobil Chatham* depart for the Chathams on what was to be an interesting voyage. (Photographs by M. Berthold, Wellington Maritime Museum Collection)

Hinunui was built on the banks of the Opawa River, a tributary of the Wairau River that runs into Cloudy Bay. Launching the *Hinunui* was a simple exercise, as it was rolled down the river bank into the river, after a launching ceremony, where Mrs Pattie Perano, wife of the founder of the Perano whaling station, officiated. The tanker was eventually towed down stream by a launch belonging to T. Eckford & Co. Ltd, who had a long association with the Marlborough and Wellington regions, owning a number of small cargo ships, which included the *Echo*, now beached at Picton.

After the tanker was clear of the Wairau Bar, the *Tuatea*, another vessel belonging to the Peranos, towed the vessel to Tory Channel. It was not long before the vessel was put into service transferring whale oil. When not required, the *Hinunui* was beached near the whale factory until the next vessel called for a load of oil.

On 21 December 1964, and after 53 years in the whaling industry, Peranos caught their last whale. Economic pressure and low whale oil prices world-wide contributed to the operation's demise. Whales had become harder to find in the area traditionally hunted by the Peranos. It was felt at the time that Russian and Japanese involvement in the industry had seriously affected the numbers of whales passing through Cook Strait.

The whale station was closed at the end of the year. The *Hinunui* transferred its last load of whale oil in mid-February 1965 to a Dutch vessel. Vessels and some equipment were sold and among the vessels put up for sale was the *Hinunui*. However, it was not until late 1967 that the *Hinunui* was sold. At this time Mobil Oil NZ Ltd were considering improvements for the supply of fuel to the growing number of fishing vessels now gathering at the Chatham Islands due to the crayfish 'boom'.

Albert Meo of the Wellington Trawling Company (which had commercial interests at the Chathams), suggested to the Fleet and Programmes Manager for Mobil Oil, Brian

The coaster *Te Aroha* with the *Hinunui* alongside approaching Shelly Bay Wharf at Wellington. (Photograph by M. Berthold, Wellington Maritime Museum Collection)

Mountjoy, that the *Hinunui* could prove useful as a fuel storage vessel at Port Hutt. Brian Mountjoy agreed and the tanker was bought for approximately $1,000. The coastal vessel *Te Aroha*, which belonged to the Karamea Shipping Company Ltd, towed the *Hinunui* from Tory Channel to Wellington. The tow had to be carried out in favourable conditions as the tanker was empty and thus sluggish and hard to handle.

Arrangements were made to slip the *Hinunui* at the Shelly Bay slipway, where it spent some months being overhauled and painted. Certain alterations were also made in preparation for the *Hinunui*'s new lease of life. Mobil changed the name to *Mobil Chatham* and registered it as a "dumb barge".

When the overhaul was complete, the *Mobil Chatham* was shifted to the eastern side of the rail ferry terminal where it was loaded with fuel in preparation for the voyage to the Chatham Islands.

The vessel responsible for towing the *Mobil Chatham* to its new home was the Holm Shipping Company vessel *Holmdale*. The tow began on 20 January 1968 and took four days to complete under difficult conditions. The *Mobil Chatham* towed very badly; on a number of occasions it rolled 360 degrees and would sheer off in many different directions.

Moorings for the tanker had to be bought from the navy which had surplus anchors and anchor cable stored at Islington Bay, on Mototapu Island, in the Hauraki Gulf. The anchors and cable had to be railed from Auckland to Wellington and put aboard the *Holmdale*. On arrival at the Chathams, preparations were made for the *Holmdale*'s surf boat to lay the *Mobil Chatham*'s

Looking more like a submarine, the *Hinunui* sits in the slipway at Shelly Bay after its alterations have been completed. (Photograph by M. Berthold, Wellington Maritime Museum Collection)

moorings in Port Hutt.

Once the moorings had been secured and the tanker settled in its new berth, vessels soon started to arrive to load fuel. The first vessel which took on fuel found that the fuel loaded in Wellington had been contaminated by sea water which had leaked into the tanker when it was rolling over. A chemist and a fitter had to be flown to the Chatham Islands to rectify the matter.

With the arrival of the *Mobil Chatham* the storage, transfer and distribution of fuel oil became easier. Fuel oil was carried to the Chatham Islands by conventional cargo ship. At the time the *Mobil Chatham* was moored in Port Hutt and up until recent years the *Holmdale* carried fuel for the Chathams in her deep tanks. On arrival at Waitangi, the *Holmdale* would discharge goods and fuel. The fuel was transferred to a 30,000 gallon tank on Tiki Tiki Hill above Waitangi Wharf. (In the early 1970s the tank was shifted down to the waterfront due to land movement.) Fuel was also transferred to the *Mobil Chatham* which was towed to a mooring at Waitangi and then returned to Port Hutt. The *Holmdale* would also pump fuel into storage facilities at Kaingaroa and occasionally at Pitt Island.

The person responsible for looking after the *Mobil Chatham* at Port Hutt was Jimmy Lenaghan, who was the manager of the Packing Company freezer at Port Hutt. Two vessels could be refuelled alongside the *Mobil Chatham* and this took some pressure of the refuelling facilities at Waitangi Wharf.

By the early 1970s the crayfish boom had come to an end and the lack of crayfish caused the Packing Company factory at Port Hutt to close. The pressure on fuel supply also eased with the majority of the large fleet of crayfishing vessels returning to their respective home ports on New Zealand.

The *Mobil Chatham* once again became surplus to requirements and was towed to Waitangi where it was beached near the fuel tank on the Waitangi foreshore to quietly rust away.

The marketing of fuels at the Chatham Islands was and still is a very expensive commodity; this imposes one of the greatest disadvantages compared with mainland New Zealand. The Islands rely heavily on a steady fuel supply for the production of electricity, transport and to run the fishing industry. The *Mobil Chatham* may seem like an insignificant vessel to most, but to the people of the Chathams and the fishermen who relied on it to refuel their vessels, it was an important link in enabling them to go about their business.

References

Marlborough Express
D. Grady, *The Perano Whalers of Cook Strait 1911-1964*, 1982

Acknowledgements

R.J. McDougall
R. Manning
B. Mountjoy

Chapter Twelve
The *Nora Niven* – a pioneer

The steam trawler *Nora Niven* was built in 1906 at Selby, England, by Cochrane and Sons Ltd for the New Zealand Trawling and Fish Supply Company Ltd of Napier. It cost £10,210, delivered to New Zealand and was the first British built steam trawler constructed for a New Zealand fishing company. A distinctive feature of its equipment was a refrigerating plant to keep the fish in cold storage. At the time no British trawler had this facility, so in this respect the *Nora Niven* was a pioneer. It was constructed in such a way that, should it have not proven a success in the fishing venture, it could easily have been converted into a small cargo vessel.

The company's much respected managing director, Mr Jas. J. Niven, went to England to superintend the construction and dispatch of the vessel to New Zealand. At a reception held at Dunedin prior to his departure, he was presented with gifts and given the honour of naming the vessel after

The 166-ton *Nora Niven*, a most modern and well-appointed steam trawler in its day. It was New Zealand's first purpose built trawler. It is seen here berthed at Wellington. (Wellington Maritime Museum Collection)

The Nora Niven – a pioneer

Nora Niven on the fishing grounds as seen from the *Futurist*. (Wellington Maritime Museum Collection)

his youngest daughter Nora.

The company believed it was embarking on an enterprise with great possibilities for the country though it involved a big risk and heavy expense to test the New Zealand fishing grounds. They had no doubt that if they were successful others would follow their lead and the industry would grow and provide employment for a considerable number of people (how right they were).

The government agreed and provided the company with a £2,500 subsidy on the condition that *Nora Niven* be made available for charter by the government for the exploration of new fishing grounds around New Zealand. This made the *Nora Niven* New Zealand's first large fisheries research vessel, although on a part time basis. Prior to this a small vessel called the *Doto* was used but it was unable to work very far from the coast.

During late January 1907 the *Nora Niven* underwent its trials, which proved in every way satisfactory. It steamed at 9 knots over the measured mile and appeared a seaworthy craft. Its skipper on the delivery voyage was Captain McAlister of Napier and a crew of eleven Grimsby fishermen were signed on. They later remained in New Zealand to give the venture a good start. The outward appearance of the vessel was that of the majority of Grimsby trawlers of the time. It was 105 feet long, 20 feet wide with a draught of 11 feet and a triple expansion engine. Under normal conditions it carried 12 days supply of coal though on the delivery voyage it also carried coal down in the fish hold. The fish capacity was 100 tons.

Some of *Nora Niven*'s officers and crew: From left to right: Chas Omers (Fishing mate), Captain Neilson (Fishing master) and Captain McAllister, who delivered the *Nora Niven* to New Zealand. Front row: F. Kemp, G. Neil, and Chas Anderson (fishermen). (*The New Zealand Graphic*)

Nora Niven arrived at Napier on 8 May 1907 from Grimsby after a voyage of approximately 70 days. It was then slipped at Wellington on the patent slip and prepared for its first trawling expedition for the government, who had chartered it for three months. All information gathered was to be made available to interested parties and the fish caught was to be sold to the owners by the Marine Department at market rates. Its first trip included the stretch of water between Lyttelton and the Chatham Islands which, as we know now, is an area rich in fish stocks. Thus began the *Nora*'s long fishing career. During the early years it made experimental voyages all around the coast and the information gathered helped to develop the fishing industry in New Zealand.

In October 1910 the newly established Chatham Island Fishing Company, engaged the *Nora Niven* to carry frozen blue cod to Wellington and Napier for a six month period. During this time it continued fishing between trips to the Chatham Islands.

During World War I it performed minesweeping duties from February 1918 to May 1919. It again served as a minesweeper during World War II, in June and July 1940, though by this time age had taken its toll and it was decided to return it to the owners to resume fishing. In 1942 the *Nora Niven* was again taken up by the Navy for duties as a danlaying vessel, but it proved to be unsatisfactory in this role and was again returned to the owners.

During its long career the *Nora Niven* was owned by three companies: New Zealand Trawling and Fish Supply Company Ltd, Napier 1907-1930; New Zealand Fisheries Ltd, Wellington 1930-1942 and National Mortgage and Agency Co Ltd, Dunedin 1944-1947. After 40 years of fishing *Nora Niven* came to the end of its career. After being partly dismantled at Port Chalmers it was towed to sea and sunk 15 miles east off Taiaroa Head in February 1947.

The industry has come a long way since the early exploratory voyages of the *Nora Niven*, but the early work of vessels like the *Nora* (an advanced vessel for the time) can be compared with the high-tech vessels of today, finding and developing the new fishing grounds which are so important to the industry and the major contribution it makes to New Zealand's economy.

Sorting fish on deck. (Wellington Maritime Museum)

Acknowledgements

This project started about three years ago, after the Wellington Maritime Museum was invited to mount a display featuring aspects of New Zealand's commercial fishing history at the trade show, FISHEX, which was held at Palmerston North in 1993. The response by visitors to the museum's display at the show was extremely positive, and many people felt their history had been overlooked for too long. On returning to Wellington I reported this to the museum's director, Ken Scadden, and after some discussion we decided to embark on a project of collecting material and oral histories relating to the fishing industry.

At about the same time the editor of *Seafood New Zealand* magazine, Peter Stevens, gave me the opportunity of submitting an article for the industry's magazine. I initially thought this was a one-off situation, but three years later the project is still going strong, thanks to his encouragement and support.

I would like to offer my thanks and gratitude to all the people who have made this book possible, particularly those generous people who allowed me to interview them, after only a brief period to allow both parties to feel at ease with each other. It is difficult to invite a stranger into your home and open your mind to them, but these people made me feel both welcome and privileged to hear their stories.

I would also like to thank Ken Scadden, who has been very patient, positive and helpful throughout this exercise. One person who has been invaluable to me during the time I have been putting this material together is my colleague, Wendy Adlam, her word processing and editing skills are very much appreciated, as is Peter Attwell, who has also assisted with editing, and my other colleagues. My thanks also to Peter Talley and Stuart Dixon of Talley's Fisheries Ltd, David Anderson and Beverley Wrend of Sanford Ltd, and others in the industry who have assisted with information and photographs. Last but never least, I would like to thank my wife Kathy and my daughters, Katerina, Demetria and Georgina, for their encouragement and support.

Emmanuel Makarios

Contained in Volume Two –

- Bluff Oyster Fishing – the *Karaka*
- The *Baroona* – a vessel of elegant beginnings
- The *Hautapu* – the ship that in the end no one wanted
- Salvaged – the *Norna*
- *Phyllis* – 42 years of chequered history
- The loss of the *Duco*
- The *Manuka* – a view from the engine room
- Fishing at Napier
- and more

The Author

Emmanuel Makarios' interest in matters maritime began in his early teens; growing up in Island Bay in Wellington, he found himself drawn to the small fishing fleet based there, and it was inevitable that he soon became acquainted with some of the fishermen who worked from the bay or the port of Wellington.

To discourage him from pursuing a career at sea, his parents sought the assistance of one of the neighbours, an Italian fisherman, to take him fishing whenever possible, in the hope that he would get so seasick he would look for a job ashore!

He saw this as a challenge however, and would happily get up in the early hours of the morning, after little or no sleep due to excitement and anticipation of the trip ahead. Although he was, at times, quite violently seasick, he found watching and helping these Italian fishermen fascinating and a real education in boat handling and seamanship.

As he approached the end of his time at college, he was offered the opportunity to go fishing but had his mind set on a career in the merchant navy. However, he has always remained fascinated by the fishing industry, with its colourful characters who worked in such harsh and dangerous conditions, in an occupation which dates back to before Biblical times.

While in the merchant navy Emmanuel served as a seaman, quartermaster and bosun on a variety of vessels.

In 1986 he joined the Wellington Maritime Museum, then operated by the Wellington Harbour Board. He is now the Museum's Exhibitions Officer.

As well as articles for *Seafood New Zealand*, he regularly contributes to the New Zealand Ship and Marine Society's publication *Marine News*.